Practical Stylistics:

an approach to poetry

H.G. Widdowson

Oxford University Press 1992

Oxford University Press
Walton Street, Oxford OX2 6DP

Oxford New York Toronto
Delhi Bombay Calcutta Madras Karachi
Petaling Jaya Singapore Hong Kong Tokyo
Nairobi Dar es Salaam Cape Town
Melbourne Auckland

and associated companies in
Berlin Ibadan

OXFORD and OXFORD ENGLISH are trade marks of Oxford University Press

ISBN 0 19 437184 0

Set in 10pt Sabon
Typeset by Tradespools Ltd, Frome, Somerset
Printed in Hong Kong

To my sister Jennifer

Contents

Acknowledgements

The author and publishers are grateful for permission to reproduce poems and extracts from poems from the following copyright material,

Anon., 'Mary Ann Lowder'. Reprinted by permission of Penguin Books Ltd.
W.H. Auden, 'Letter to Lord Byron', 'Heavy Date', and 'Lay your sleeping head'. Reprinted by permission of Faber & Faber Ltd.
e.e. Cummings, 'one' and 'Me up at does'. Reprinted by permission of HarperCollins Publishers and Liveright Publishing Corporation.
T.S. Eliot, 'The Waste Land' and 'Journey of the Magi'. Reprinted by permission of Faber & Faber Ltd and Harcourt Brace Jovanovich.
D.J. Enright, 'Paradise Illustrated'. Reprinted by permission of Watson, Little Ltd.
Robert Frost, 'Fireflies in the Garden' and 'Dust of Snow'. Reprinted by permission of Jonathan Cape Ltd and Henry Holt & Co.
Robert Graves, 'Flying Crooked' and 'Love without Hope'. Reprinted by permission of A.P. Watt Ltd and Oxford University Press (NY).
Seamus Heaney, 'Mother of the Groom'. Reprinted by permission of Faber & Faber Ltd and Farrar, Straus & Giroux Inc.
Philip Larkin, 'At Grass'. Reprinted by permission of The Marvell Press. 'Ambulances', 'The Trees', and 'As Bad as a Mile'. Reprinted by permission of Faber & Faber Ltd and Farrar, Straus & Giroux Inc.
Ogden Nash, 'Beneath this slab'. Reprinted by permission of Curtis Brown Ltd, Little Brown & Co Inc, and J.M. Dent & Sons Ltd.
Theodore Roethke, 'Night Crow'. Reprinted by permission of Faber & Faber Ltd and Doubleday.
Siegfried Sassoon, 'Everyone Sang' and 'Base Details'. Reprinted by permission of George Sassoon and Viking Penguin Inc.
Wallace Stevens, 'Metaphors of a Magnifico'. Reprinted by permission of Faber & Faber Ltd and A.A. Knopf Inc.
William Carlos Williams, 'This Is Just to Say', 'The Red Wheelbarrow', and 'The Locust Tree in Flower'. Florence Williams, 'Reply'. Reprinted by permission of Carcanet Press Ltd and New Directions Publishing.

Every effort has been made to trace the owners of the following copyright material, but the publishers would be pleased to hear from any copyright holder whom they have been unable to contact,

The poems 'Beauty' by Matsuo Basho and 'Spring' by Kobayashi Issa, both translated by Harold G. Henderson. The poem 'Railwaymen' by Raymond Richardson. The poem 'Revolver' by Alan Riddell. The poem 'Nature's Miracles' by Patience Strong. The poem 'New Corn' by T'ao Ch'ien, translated by Arthur Waley. The poem 'Mind' by Richard Wilbur.

Introduction

In this book I present a view about the nature of poetry as a use of language, suggest the relevance of this view for education, and demonstrate how it might be acted upon in pedagogic practice. As such, it can be read as a development of ideas about stylistic analysis and its application expressed in my previous book (Widdowson 1975). It has been suggested that what I have to say is really a version of the old (and for many, discredited) ideas associated with Practical Criticism, dressed up deceptively in stylistic guise to give the appearance of novelty. Naturally I would deny this, although I acknowledge that there are resemblances. It would be appropriate, therefore, to indicate in this introduction how the view I take relates to that of other lines of thought in literary criticism.

The very title of this book invokes—or provokes rather, since it is a matter of deliberate design—the notion of Practical Criticism, the approach to the interpretation of poetry first proposed by I.A. Richards. This approach, brilliantly exemplified by the work of Richards' pupil William Empson (1930–1961), became established as an orthodoxy, sustained by such influential books as Cox and Dyson 1963 and 1965, each reprinted several times over the years. The question arises as to how this approach differs from that which I adopt here under the name of Practical Stylistics.

In both approaches the poetic text is considered in dissociation from context and subjected to close scrutiny in the search for its significance. But where is this significance to be found? There are three possibilities. It might be found in using the text as evidence of writer intention: what is significant is what the writer means by the text. Alternatively, one might take the view that the text signals its own intrinsic meaning, whatever the writer might have intended: what is significant is what the text means. Or, thirdly, one might say that what is significant is what a text means to the reader, whatever the writer may have intended, or whatever the text itself may objectively appear to mean.

Practical Criticism wavers between these three positions. Sometimes it looks as if it is directed at discovering the intrinsic meaning contained within the text, its semantic content. Thus Richards talks about respecting the autonomy of the poem (Richards 1929:277), and cautions against the intrusion of idiosyncratic readings, as evidenced by the reactions of his own students. Similarly, Cox and Dyson talk about poems as if they had their own independent organic life:

> A poem that is in any degree successful blossoms under our careful attention, and comes into fullness as we proceed.
> (Cox and Dyson 1965:12)

Analysis, they say, reveals the poem's 'totality' so that reading it

> ... includes a new sense of the poem's structure and imagery, its tone and verbal delicacy, its precise effects.
> (ibid.:13)

The implication seems to be that these effects are the property of the poem itself as an autonomous artefact and are in principle recoverable from the text, totally and intact. Nevertheless, there is an acknowledgement that an author is lurking somewhere in the background and that meaning has something to do with his (*sic*) intentions:

> The poet writing the poem has certainly been conscious of many effects he precisely intended.
> (ibid.:13)

One cannot help noticing how non-committal this statement is in its curious wording. Surely the poet would have been conscious, necessarily, of *all* effects he precisely intended. And what if he is? Are the effects to be recovered those which were intended, or those which are intrinsic to the text as an autonomous totality?

For other critics, notably those in the tradition of New Criticism, any consideration of author intention is a fallacy. Their concern is emphatically with what the text means and not with what the author means by the text. Nor are they concerned with what the text might mean to the reader. This too is a distraction, another fallacy. Thus Wimsatt:

> The Intentional Fallacy is a confusion between the poem and its origins ... It begins by trying to derive the standard of criticism

from the psychological *causes* of the poem and ends in
biography and relativism. The Affective Fallacy is a confusion
between the poem and its *results* (what it *is* and what it
does . . .). It begins by trying to derive the standard of criticism
from the psychological effects of the poem and ends in
impressionism and relativism. The outcome of either fallacy,
the Intentional or the Affective, is that the poem itself, as an
object of specifically critical judgement, tends to disappear.
(Wimsatt 1970:21)

The poem itself, as it *is*, its essential being: this is the object of literary study. It would seem that the effects that Cox and Dyson
speak of, even those emanating as results from the text itself, are
to be eliminated from consideration. What counts is what the text
means, and nothing else.

But of course what the text means has to be apprehended. You
can get rid of the writer and consider a text in complete dissociation from the conditions of its production. But reception is
another matter. The only meaning that a text can have is what is
read into it by the receiver. On its own it is simply an inert object.
You cannot eliminate the reader, for the reader is the only agent
whereby meaning can be activated. The essential issue is what role
the agent is to play.

Generally speaking in Practical Criticism the reader is cast in a
subservient and submissive role: the task is to *discover* the meanings which are immanent in the text. Distinctions made by Goffman are relevant here. He points out (Goffman 1981) that the
producer of language (speaker or writer) may simply be making
manifest somebody else's script, acting as a mouthpiece, an *animator* and not an *author*. Or the producer may be author, but an
author with limited initiative, acting on the dictates of some other
authority, responsible for the wording of the text but not for the
ideas it expresses: author but not *principal*. These distinctions can
be applied at the reception end of the communication process as
well. Thus the reader can assume the role of animator, whose task
is simply to activate meanings deemed to be in the text, but who
takes no initiative to engage creatively with the text and so to act
as author of personal reaction. As animator, we might say, the
reader provides an exegesis. As author, the reader provides an
interpretation.

But the animator role in this receptive sense requires a great deal of special expertise in the reading of signs and the assigning of significance. Exegesis is an élite and privileged activity, reserved for such people as scholars and priests. Anybody can provide an interpretation based on personal reaction. So it is that typically in Practical Criticism we find the autonomy of the text combined with the authority of the critic, each a guarantee of the other.

Though this position, this positioning of the reader as animator of the text, still seems to be the prevailing orthodoxy in literature teaching, it has been called into question over the past fifteen years or so. The reader has been cast in the role of author. This shift results in what Fish calls Affective Stylistics (Fish 1980) or what is most commonly known as Reader–Response Criticism (Freund 1987). The title of Freund's book is *The Return of the Reader*; but it is not so much that the reader has returned, for he or she was always and inevitably there, but that the role has changed. Reading is seen now not as a matter of submitting to the authority of the text so as to provide an exegesis of its integral meaning, but of asserting an interpretation on the reader's own authority. You do not read meanings out of a text but into a text. A problem then arises about interpretative promiscuity. How do you prevent individual readers authorizing *any* meaning no matter how idiosyncratic? One answer is to socialize the reader by making him or her representative of a group sharing the same basic ideology, the same schematic set of assumptions, beliefs, values, etc. In other words, you cast the reader in the role of principal so that the significance assigned to the text carries with it what Fish calls (in the subtitle of his book) *The authority of interpretive communities*. Hence the reader interprets a text not as an individual but as a member of, say, a Marxist or a feminist community.

Where, then, do I stand in relation to these perspectives? Essentially, I argue that the experience of poetry, and its educational relevance, depend on the reader assuming an author role. For me, meaning is not in the text, to be animated by the expert reader. But equally, it is not derived from the text by the socialized reader acting as principal and representative of some ideologically informed interpretative community. In both of these cases, it seems to me, you deny the divergence of individual interpretation and defer to the judgement of an informed élite. The essential elusiveness of poetic meaning is thereby fixed, and falsified.

But people will surely come up with diverse and divergent interpretations anyway. They hardly need to be encouraged to do so. What, then, is the teaching of poetry to do, if not to acquaint students with the exegesis of expert animators, or with the evaluations of principals of a particular ideological persuasion? My answer would be: to provide them with ways of justifying their own judgement by making as precise reference to the text as possible.

It is important to note that I am talking about precision of reference to the text in support of a particular interpretation. What I am emphatically not talking about is precision of interpretation itself. This is a distinction which is crucial to my argument, and central to the purpose of this book, so it would be as well to dwell on it for a moment.

In the introduction to the Cox and Dyson textbook on the practical criticism of poetry, reference is made (as I have already noted) to the 'precise effects' of a poem. 'This precision', the authors say, 'is what practical criticism exists to achieve' (ibid.:13). But the effects of poetry are never precise: they are evocative, suggestive, allusive—elusive indeed. If they were made precise, they would become referential. The poem would then simply conform to the normal conditions of conventional statement and lose its point. We can, however, be precise about what it is in the poetic text which induces us to read a particular meaning into it. In other words, precision is appropriate in identifying cause in the text, but not in describing the effect on the reader. And it is this, I would suggest, that is distinctive about the practical stylistic approach that I propose in this book.

Consider one example: comments made in Cox and Dyson (1963) about Philip Larkin's poem *At Grass* about racehorses in retirement:

> The old racehorses in this poem are first seen lost in shadow, almost undistinguishable until the wind moves a tail or mane. Using only very simple words, Larkin invests this situation with a richness of emotional effects. The horses seem to be fading into death, their unique identities slipping back to the darkness from which they came. We are reminded of the pathos of old age and the swift passing of time. It is as if the horses were the shades of all human ambitions and triumphs. They have left behind them all that gave significance to their lives. Their movements have no meaning; one *seems* to look at the other, but probably sees nothing. No purpose gives them an identity,

or rescues them from anonymity. It is as if all existence proceeds in the same direction, as time wastes away the shapes we have tried to make out of our lives.
(Cox and Dyson 1963:138)

Here the effects of the poem on a particular reader are stated very precisely indeed. What is imprecise, indeed virtually non-existent, is any reference to what it is in the actual language of the text which gives warrant to this impressionistic account of what the poem means to these readers. We are told that Larkin uses only very simple words. How is the concept 'simple word' to be defined? The second verse of the poem, for example, runs as follows:

Yet fifteen years ago, perhaps
Two dozen distances sufficed
To fable them: faint afternoons
Of Cups and Stakes and Handicaps,
Whereby their names were artificed
To inlay faded, classic Junes—

Are these words really only very simple ones? If they are, the criteria for simplicity are not at all obvious. And just how do these words, simple or not, have the effect claimed for them? What is it about them that 'invests this situation with a richness of emotional effects'? To pose such questions is not to deny the validity of this particular interpretation (or any other, for that matter) but to ask what textual evidence might be adduced to provide it with validation. Many of the observations that Cox and Dyson make are very persuasive. Given their academic prestige, this is hardly surprising: they speak with authority. And that is, precisely, the problem. Students are likely to be convinced into conformity and to accept their interpretations as definitive, or at least more authoritative than their own. It is not difficult to imagine the phrases in the passage I quoted earlier cropping up in essays and examination answers. And so it is that students are encouraged to put their trust in the secondary texts of literary criticism (the study guides and notes that are published in such profusion) and discouraged from engaging with the primary texts of the poems themselves. Thus students are assigned the role of animators, mouthing the authorial or principal judgements of others, not acting as interpretative authors in their own right.

The approach I propose in this book seeks to stimulate an engagement with primary texts, to encourage individual interpretation while requiring that this should be referred back to features of the text. What is important here is not the interpretation itself, but the process of exploration of meaning; not the assertion of effects but the investigation into the linguistic features which seem to give warrant to these effects.

This exploration is itself a fascinating experience and I have tried to draw the reader into participating in the pleasure that I find in it myself. For this reason I have presented the discussion in the first part of the book as an unfolding personal narrative of enquiry rather than as an argument of a standard academic kind located in the theoretical context of scholarly thought. I have provided this context separately in the notes, which are, therefore, rather more extensive than is customary. These notes also acknowledge the contribution made by the ideas and practices of other people who have been working on an approach to pedagogy which integrates the study of language and literature.

But there are other acknowledgements to be made as well. The book has emerged over the years from courses I have taught in London at the Institute of Education, and on Summer Institutes in Tokyo, Barcelona, Flagstaff, and Georgetown. I am grateful to the participants on these courses for their comments and encouragement. I am grateful, too, for the stimulation and support that I have received from my colleagues in the profession: my thanks in particular to Christopher Brumfit, Ron Carter, Guy Cook, Alan Maley, and Andy Murison-Bowie, all of whom commented on an earlier draft of this book. Some were negative about it, some positive, but all had valuable points to make which I have taken note of (though not necessarily acted upon) in the revision. My thanks also to Jennifer Bassett for her detailed comments on the last draft, based on both editorial expertise and literary perception.

Finally, a special word of thanks to Sybil Spence: not only for her care and skill in preparing the book for publication, but for all her consideration and support.

H.G. Widdowson
London, August 1991

PART ONE

The significance of poetry

1   To begin with: common features and uncouth rhymes

There are nine and sixty ways of constructing tribal lays
And–every–single–one–of–them–is–right!
(Kipling: *In the Neolithic Age*)

And there are no doubt nine and sixty ways of describing the nature of poetry and accounting for its significance: theoretical constructs, all designed to demonstrate by argument that they are right (and others wrong). But they are all ultimately based on individual attitude. We rationalize our subjective dispositions so as to persuade others to accept them as having more general validity. My own account is no exception. It seems appropriate, therefore, to set it right away in a personal key ...

The birth of this book had its beginning among the dead. During a convalescence after surgery, I began my cautious way back to health by taking daily walks in a neighbouring cemetery. This was a place conveniently close to home and provided a kind of purpose. So it was preferable to pointless wandering around the streets. Besides, such a place was appropriate to the relieved and reflective convalescent mood; a place, as Philip Larkin puts it, which was 'proper to grow wise in'.

The gravestones bear the record of bereavement. Sometimes all that is left of love and grief, so overwhelming in the immediate moment, is an engraved trace in simple words: *died, fell asleep, passed away, called to rest.* The conventional euphemisms are only token attempts to disguise this awful final deprivation. Sometimes, though, the bereaved turn to poetry for solace and significance. Usually it is not very impressive poetry by any aesthetic standards. It is crude verbal carving. It can be dismissed as doggerel. And yet, these faltering and faulty attempts at giving shape to sorrow reveal a good deal about the essential nature of poetic art.

His memory is as dear today
As in the hour he passed away.
(Ernest C. Draper 'Ern'. Died 4.1.38)

> There is a link death cannot sever,
> Love and remembrance live for ever.
> (John Reed. Died 14.10.56)

But of course all this cannot be true. Who now, today, remembers Ernest C. Draper as the person affectionately known to family and friends as Ern? Love and remembrance do not live for ever; they fade in the minds of the living until they die in their turn. All graves in time are left untended and their tenants forgotten. Why then do we record such falsehood permanently in stone? It can only be that at the time they are not felt as falsehoods, but as true to some sense of reality which is not accountable to conventional conditions of truth. They are expressions of conviction at a different level of awareness. And of course the fact that I, as a complete stranger, can now, thirty-five years, fifty-odd years into the future, read these lines means that in a sense the love and remembrance which prompted their composition do live on, and live for as long as the gravestone remains. Today as recorded on the fourth of January 1938 has some sort of common reference to today as I read these lines. The very recording of the falsehood ensures its survival as a kind of truth which exists in a different dimension, and not subject to conventional concepts of time. One point about poetry is that it outlives and transcends the occasion of its composition, and transfers its significance in some way to strangers in another time and place.

> Day by day we all do miss her.
> Words would fail our loss to tell.
> But in heaven we hope to meet her,
> Evermore with her to dwell.
> (Daisy Hillier. Died 1.4.50)

Here is one answer to the problem of truth and permanence: we shift into the plane of religious reality. Heaven by definition is an absolute, set apart and existing for ever. Poetry as an attempt to capture what is fleeting coexists with different and institutionalized formulations of other worlds. It interrelates with established belief. The lines here have the resonances of a Christian hymn. The text on the gravestone carries the sound of church singing, and this too is part of its meaning. As with all poems, this one vibrates with intertextual implication, for all poetry is a kind of reverberation of endless echoes.

There is, then, in this verse a certain alignment with orthodox religion. But this co-occurs with unorthodox reasoning. Consider the second line:

Words would fail our loss to tell.

But this is a contradiction: the words *do* tell the loss. The logical implication of the line is denied in its very expression. Words would fail, so we will not use them. But we do use them nevertheless, and so they do not actually fail. There is a paradox here that cannot be rationally resolved. Again, this seems to be a feature of poetry in general: it cannot be interpreted by a direct application of conventional logic. Since it is expressive of some elusive reality outside the confines of what is conventional, this is hardly surprising. In these particular lines, the expression of religious conformity, which we have already noticed, coexists with a contrary expression of rational non-conformity. There is a similar disparity between the regularity of the sound patterns of the poem, its rhythm and rhyme, and the irregularity of its grammar: *Words would fail our loss to tell*, not the usual word order of *Words would fail to tell our loss*. What this seems to suggest is that to express an awareness of experience which is out of the ordinary, we need to mould ordinary language and logic into a different shape. We need to disrupt conventional patterns of thought and expression and reformulate them into patterns which follow different principles of order.

I suggest, then, that we can discern in these simple epitaphs features which are common to all poetry: the fashioning of thought and language to capture the elusive sense of reality in a different dimension, the paradoxical expression of what cannot be expressed, the verbal echoing. It is true that these are what Thomas Gray in his Elegy, that most celebrated of graveyard poems, referred to as 'uncouth rhymes'. They lack the artistry of poems which have been canonized as works of literature. It is only the stone they are carved in which gives them any permanence. None would survive in print. But the theme of Gray's Elegy is that in essentials the great and the lowly are alike, and so it is that these doggerel verses can be recognized as related to loftier instances of verbal art. They are humble kin to the sonnets of Shakespeare and the odes of Keats.

And it is important, I think, that the kinship should be recognized. The need to give poetic form to feelings which cannot be adequately contained within conventional utterance is every-where apparent in daily life. We see it in clumsy compositions of epitaphs and obituaries, in greetings cards and valentines, in popular song: the common muse. But this poetic instinct is suppressed in our schooling by a discontinuity between these uncouth rhymes and simple verses and the canonized work of established poetry. Children are confronted with a literature which is culturally distanced from them, remote and sanctified, one which they cannot relate to by reference to their own experience. It is little wonder that so many of them regard it as classroom drudgery and reject it. How many people read poetry willingly and for pleasure? The fact that they are so few is evidence of a massive educational failure.

To sanctify poetry, literature in general, is to falsify it. The only reality it will suggest is the conventional one of classroom values which call for conformity. Instead of inspiring an exploration of individual experience it will simply confirm that which is established by authority.

And with sanctity, of course, comes solemnity. And this again is a misrepresentation. The epitaphs I quoted earlier are poignant testimony to the baffled sorrow of bereavement. They deserve respect. But like all taboo topics, death can also provoke deliberate disrespect. It can be made comical, as in these commemorative lines for Sir John Vanbrugh, the celebrated eighteenth-century architect:

> Lie heavy on him earth, for he
> Laid many a heavy weight on thee.

Funeral ritual conventionally calls for social decorum, but feelings cannot be easily contained within such conventions and they will occasionally break out into irreverence, as in these ribald rhymes:

> Here lies the body of Mary Ann Lowder,
> She burst while drinking a seidlitz powder.
> Called from this world to her heavenly rest,
> She should have waited till it effervesced.
> (Anon)

> Beneath this slab
> John Brown is stowed.
> He watched the ads
> And not the road.
> (Ogden Nash)

Not all literature is solemn, then, and none of it is sacrosanct. Poetry, expressive as it is of feelings beyond what are expected and customary, may be sublime, but may also be ridiculous. And it may ridicule itself by parody. To preserve it from irreverence, and surround it with an aura of sanctity is to bestow upon it established social values which it is its very purpose to transcend.

So the expressive range and continuity of poetry which extends from obscene limerick to *Paradise Lost* should not be diminished to a set of privileged texts of aesthetic and moral probity. Both the common muse and the comic muse have essential contributions to make. Lines from W.H. Auden are relevant here:

> By all means let us touch our humble caps to
> *La poésie pure*, the epic narrative;
> But comedy shall get its round of claps too.
> According to his powers, each may give;
> Only on varied diet can we live.
> The pious fable and the dirty story
> Share in the total literary glory.
> (*Letter to Lord Byron*)

At this point it would be easy to conclude that since canonized poetry is so culturally remote and so protective of privilege it should be removed from the curriculum in favour of writing of more immediately popular appeal. But this, I believe, would be a mistaken conclusion. Literature needs to be democratized, but this is not achieved by deprivation. To deny children access to great literature is to keep it within the preserve of an élite. What needs to be done is to make it more readily accessible. So it is not a matter of *replacing* the prestigious with the popular but of developing an awareness of how they are *related*, how they share the total literary glory which everybody is entitled to experience. The task of education is to reveal their common kinship.

As I indicated earlier, one common feature of poetry is the fashioning of language to represent awareness which eludes conventional expression. The effect is to give point or poignancy to words which ultimately cannot be explained but only experienced. What happens with poetry, whether lofty or lowly, is that the customary correspondences between words and the world are disrupted and realigned.

These customary correspondences are crucial. They bind us to the world we live in, and provide us with the necessary illusions of security and control. The Bible asserts their primacy: *In the beginning was the word.* It is not, therefore, surprising that Adam's first recorded act in Genesis is the setting up of such correspondences in the naming of the animals. This is D.J. Enright's unauthorized, and unsanctified, version of the event:

> So they shuffled past, or they hopped,
> Or they waddled. The beasts of the field
> And the fowls of the air,
> Pretending not to notice him.

> 'Speak up now,' said the Lord God briskly.
> 'Give each and every one the name thereof.'

> 'Fido,' said Adam, thinking hard,
> As the animals went past him one by one,
> 'Bambi', 'Harpy', 'Pooh',
> 'Incitatus', 'Acidosis', 'Apparat',
> 'Krafft-Ebing', 'Indo-China', 'Schnorkel',
> 'Buggins', 'Bollock'—

> 'Bullock will do,' said the Lord God, 'I like it.
> The rest are rubbish. You must try again tomorrow.'
> (*Paradise Illustrated*)

Adam is not free to give his own names: he is directed by divinity. And we are all directed in upbringing to the formulation of correspondences between words and world which are recognized in our own languages. The idiosyncratic names that children give as they begin to categorize the reality around them are modified into conformity. This is the essential condition of membership of their community. In this way, individuality is subordinated to the communal values of society. What poetry does is, in some measure, to restore individuality by allowing for the expression of alternative values. The old Adam in the poet finds other names for the familiar and no Lord God or social convention can tell him he is wrong, for their writ, holy or otherwise, has no validity in his domain.

The idea that reality is essentially constituted by language is not, of course, unique to the Bible. It finds expression in other creation myths as well: those, for example, of the Australian Aborigines.

Aboriginal Creation myths tell of the legendary totemic beings
who had wandered over the continent in the Dreamtime, singing out the name of everything that crossed their path—birds,
animals, plants, rocks, waterholes—and so singing the world
into existence.
(Bruce Chatwin: *The Songlines*)

Once the world is named or sung into existence, it becomes authorized.[1] But this does not prevent us from sensing other potential worlds which might have been called into being but were not.
All presences imply absences, and our routine reality is haunted
by what could be, what should be, what might have been. What
poetry does is to explore these absences, the meanings which lie
unrealized in the interstices of conventionalized thought. It sings
other worlds into existence. And it does so by exploiting the
unused resources of language.

Poetry is the expression of all manner of imaginative insight, of
subtle thought and profound feeling, but it has no special subject
matter of its own. Although it tends to be associated in the popular mind with the grand and noble themes of the human condition, what is so often striking about it is the way it makes
significant what is conventionally considered to be insignificant,
trivial, commonplace. The content of poems, to the extent that it
can be reduced to the summary essentials of ordinary observation,
is, generally speaking, unimpressive. Time passes. Being in love is
a wonderful feeling. Nature is beautiful. Life is lonely. Very true
these truisms, and so what? But the essentials of poetry lie in the
way language is used to elaborate on such simple propositions so
that they are reformulated in unfamiliar terms which somehow
capture the underlying mystery of the commonplace.

Like as the waves make towards the pebbled shore,
So do our minutes hasten to their end ...
(Shakespeare: *Sonnets, 60*)

Love, all alike, no season knows, nor clime,
Nor hours, days, months, which are the rags of time ...
(Donne: *The Sun Rising*)

The trees are in their autumn beauty,
The woodland paths are dry,
Under the October twilight the water
Mirrors a still sky ...
(Yeats: *The Wild Swans at Coole*)

> And I, the last, go forth companionless,
> And the days darken round me, and the years,
> Among new men, strange faces, other minds ...
> (Tennyson: *Morte d'Arthur*)

And as the language is fashioned, so it brings, indeed sings, into existence new if elusive images of reality. It is essentially the language that brings them into being. And outside the language so shaped to express them they have no existence. Poems are uses of language, and they can only be understood as uses of language. But since these uses are unusual, so they have to be understood in ways which are different from those which are common in the management of ordinary life.

That is one way of putting it, one of the nine and sixty ways of constructing an account of poetry from personal disposition. And it is one which will inevitably provoke dissent. For this is not the way that others see it. Singing other worlds into existence, indeed! Elusive images of reality. Surely this is a romanticized and sentimental view which (in spite of your assertions to the contrary) puts poetry on a pedestal as a specially prestigious kind of discourse, apart from the world of ordinary affairs and so irrelevant to it. Apart from it, I would reply, but not therefore irrelevant: on the contrary, relevant, indeed, *because* it is apart; because it has to do with impressions, ideas, senses which are out of the ordinary, beyond conventional account and so not socially accountable. But they are nevertheless real enough and the individual is aware of them even if they cannot be pinned down. Such a view will not, of course, commend itself to those who believe that nothing is significant that cannot be called to social account, that no values are valid which are not communal ones, and that literature can only be understood in terms of competing ideologies, with every text a manifesto or a tract. I believe that to socialize literature in this way is to reduce it, and that its significance, and its relevance, depend on it being not politicized but personalized.[2] So, to proceed ...

2 Significance beyond plain speaking

Poems are uses of language. Like other uses of language, they are meant to be interpreted as having some relevance to human affairs. Their very appearance in print implies that they have something of significance to say. Although they may express an individual, even idiosyncratic, perception, they are not private but public statements and so make some claim to be relevant to other people's lives. There would otherwise be no point in publication. Even the verses on gravestones publicize private feelings and suggest more general significance. They are not only testimony to first-person bereavement for the second-person dead, but involve us too, as third-person witness of the event. Daisy Hillier and Ernest Draper mean nothing to me as individuals and I am unaffected by their death. But the verses imply that it should not be a matter of indifference. Their death has in itself no particular significance. But it does in what it represents. I catch the echo of my own mortality. This seems a sentimental thing to say, and so in a sense it is. But it is, in part at least, what John Donne expresses in the following passage, whose familiarity suggests that it must capture something essential in human awareness.

> Any man's *death* diminishes *me*, because I am involved in *Mankind*; And therefore never send to know for whom the *bell* tolls; It tolls for *thee*.
> (*Devotions, XVII* [Donne's italics])

At one level, of course, this is nonsense. I am not diminished at all by *any* man's death. The bell tolls for somebody else. At the *literal* level this statement cannot be true. But at a *literary* level it carries conviction. This sense of the significance, this realization of relevance, is what is expressed too in a poem by Philip Larkin. An ambulance draws up to the kerb of an ordinary street.

Then children strewn on steps or road,
Or women coming from the shops
Past smells of different dinners, see
A wild white face that overtops
Red stretcher-blankets momently
As it is carried in and stowed,

And sense the solving emptiness
That lies just under all we do,
And for a second get it whole,
So permanent and blank and true.
The fastened doors recede. *Poor soul,*
They whisper at their own distress . . .
(*Ambulances*)

However slight, particular, and ordinary the subject matter of poetry might seem to be, the very fact that it is fashioned into poetry makes it significant of something other than itself, and suggests a more general relevance.

And yet the nature of this relevance and the manner it is signified defy easy definition. Poems are uses of language, but in many ways they are peculiar uses of language. Their meanings are elliptical and elusive, deflections from the familiar. They seem often to be perversely obscure in their flouting of conventional standards of clarity and commonsense. They are frequently eccentric in choice of word and turn of phrase. They are cast in curious prosodic forms of rhythm and rhyme, assembling language not, as is usual, in sequence but in parallel lines. If they do indeed have something of significance to say, why, then, one might ask, do they do it in such devious ways? If they are relevant, why is the relevance not made more explicitly apparent?

Poetry is always in some sense perverse and its relevance lies somewhere in its perversity. It is significant because it signifies in unusual and devious ways. Poems draw attention to themselves by their very oddity, and this oddity implies the new realization of some aspect of reality by which we were previously unaffected or of which we were unaware. Here is something, they seem to say, which is in two senses out of the ordinary and which is worth thinking about.

But at the same time, of course, this oddity precludes plain speaking. It presents us with a problem to solve. But it cannot be solved by our customary ways of interpreting other uses of language, whereby we reduce what is said to our own terms, recast it so that it fits into our familiar scheme of things. We cannot simply convert the meaning of a poem into something more manageable, something more in accord with convention, by producing a prose paraphrase or statement of gist. For to do this is to change the poem's pattern, deprive it of its peculiarity and therefore of its point.

This is true even of the humble gravestone verses that we considered earlier. If we were to recast them into the prose of ordinary statement, all the sense of the extraordinary, captured in the ceremonial shaping of language, would be lost. The rhythms, the rhymes, the vertical arrangement of verse, the particular choice of words, the abnormality of word order, all in some way *mean* something, though one may be at a loss to know just what it is. There is something here that cannot be explained because it cannot be expressed in other terms.

But at the same time we cannot make great claims for these simple compositions of the common muse. Their contribution to the common literary glory is surely small. They exemplify the need and nature of poetry as a mode of expression, but the actual meanings they express are usually too close to established ritual sentiment to stimulate the estrangement from the familiar which we usually associate with poetry. And here we have another problem to solve: the mystery of varying aesthetic response. Why is it that one combination of words somehow strikes the right key, reverberates with a subtle suggestiveness, and another stays dull and flat? In both cases we can know what *kind* of response is appropriate, and so recognize the common poetic features which make them kin, but the *quality* of response is different.

There is a parallel here with jokes, another use of language which disrupts the patterns of conventional expectation. We can recognize the intention to amuse, and the devices which are used to achieve that effect, and so identify the joke as a verbal event. But we may still fail to find it funny. We find some jokes funnier than others and some not funny at all. Similarly, we find some poems more affecting than others and some with no affect whatever. Why? Still on the theme of epitaphs, we might compare the examples from the cemetery that I gave earlier with the following two lines 'Upon the death of Sir Albert Morton's Wife', written by the seventeenth-century poet Sir Henry Wotton (I have modernized the spelling):

He first deceased; she for a little tried
To live without him: liked it not, and died.

I find these lines very moving, and the fact that they have been
widely anthologized suggests that others are similarly affected.
They express some subtlety of meaning, some undefinable significance, which the other obituary verses do not. But is it entirely
undefinable? There must be some way in which we can account, at
least in part, for this difference of aesthetic effect. At all events, an
account of the nature of poetry needs to make the attempt.

We need, then, not only to identify defining features to describe
poetry in general as a mode of expression, but we also need to
relate these to the distinguishing features of particular poems
which provide us with some basis for evaluation. An account
which denied the common poetic character of lofty and lowly
verse would be suspect. But so too would one which failed to
allow for any aesthetic distinction to be made between, say,
Donne's divine sonnets and doggerel.

Poems, then, somehow make out-of-the-ordinary meanings of
varying subtlety of sense and force out of ordinary events and experiences. These meanings are of their nature only accessible by
using procedures of interpretation other than those we usually
employ in our understanding of language. At the same time, such
procedures clearly cannot be completely dissociated from our
normal practices, for then there could be no basis for interpretation at all. Whatever is new can only be recognized by reference to
what is known. When confronted with a poem, our first inclina-
tion perhaps is to read it as we would any other communication,
looking for meanings which we can accommodate within our customary scheme of things, rather in the same way as we look for
something in a painting which we can recognize as replicating the
familiar world. Only when these normal procedures are baffled by
abnormality do we recognize the need to extend them in some
way and take a somewhat different perspective. After all, the very
appearance of the poem on the page, its vertical arrangement of
language in parallel lines, suggests that it needs to be read in a particular way. Many readers will, of course, resist the suggestion, be
disinclined to make the effort, and will not want to go beyond
what can be transposed into conventional terms. Others will be
prepared to be drawn into the poem and be ready to adapt to its
demands, attracted perhaps by a certain cadence or particular

image, intrigued to know how these might contribute to some underlying coherence made out of meanings along other dimensions beyond those which are immediately apparent.

3 Procedures for interpretation: reference and representation

What procedures might then be employed for the interpretation of poetry? We can begin our enquiry into the question by considering a short and seemingly simple poem by W.B. Yeats. Its theme is appropriate in that it refers us back once more to the gravestone inscriptions with which we began.

Memory

One had a lovely face,
And two or three had charm,
But charm and face were in vain
Because the mountain grass
Cannot but keep the form
Where the mountain hare has lain.

The first impression we get as we read the poem is that the meaning seems to pass us by, fleeting and elusive, like images seen from a moving train, and we arrive at the end of the poem without any clear idea of what has actually been said: something about faces and charm and mountain grass and mountain hare. Something catches at the mind, but what exactly? We return, replay the poem, try to get it into focus by recurrent reading. This initial elusiveness, and the refocusing that it provokes, are, of course, part of the significance of the poem, because they are phases in our experience of its meaning. If we now hold the poem still and look at it more closely, what features come into focus?

We are presented with a complex proposition contained within a single orthographic sentence. We customarily process written language by taking such orthographic sentences (consisting as they might of several grammatical sentences) as units of meaning, assuming that whatever is incomplete or unclear will be resolved by reference to other sentences coming before or after, or to some knowledge of the external context—who produced the sentence, when, where, and under what circumstances. It is because such assumptions prove to be mistaken on this occasion that we find ourselves suddenly stranded at the end of our first reading. For this sentence is self-contained and makes no connection. We do not know the contextual conditions of its composition. It follows from nothing that has preceded and anticipates nothing in the way of continuity. It comes out of the blue and it goes nowhere. We have a number of related propositions arranged syntactically as a series of clauses comprising one orthographic sentence, and arranged prosodically as six lines of verse. And that is all. It is because it is so cut off, thus denying us the usual recourse to cross-reference, that we are prompted to return to the poem to find out what we might have missed on the first time round. And this incitement to re-reading carries the implicit claim that what we missed is particularly significant, and well worth returning for. Poems suggest significance to the extent that they do not signify in customary linguistic ways. Of course, we can always resist this prompting of the poem and refuse to re-read. We can be frustrated rather than stimulated by its initial effect, and abandon efforts at understanding. This reaction is, of course, very common in class-rooms. The purpose of this book is to suggest ways in which frustration might be converted to stimulation, and the first move is to make clear what procedures of interpretation are implied by the very nature of poetic discourse.

We return now to this particular poem. Whatever it says lays claim to be significant and coherent as a self-contained and self-sufficient statement of one sort or another. So what *does* it say? Let us try to get its meaning into focus. We know in general what it is about because the title tells us: memory; not *a* memory, or *the* memory, or memor*ies*. On the most natural interpretation, there-fore, the poem is about the capacity for remembering, not any particular remembrance. So the title primes the reader to expect the poem to say something about the nature of memory in general. What, then, according to the poem, *is* memory?

It is not at all clear. To begin with, having been primed by the title to expect some general statement of some sort about memory in general, we first encounter particular remembrances of individ-ual people. Only in the second half of the poem is the expectation prompted by the title actually satisfied, by the assumption that memory is likened to the trace of the hare in the mountain grass.

This is a striking image, but an elusive one. For how does it represent a generalization based on what is said in the rest of the poem? And why does it appear in the second three lines and not at the beginning where the title might lead us to expect it? We might try to adjust the poem so that it does conform more closely to this expectation and make the connection between the general nature of memory and particular remembrances more explicit.

Memory

Memory is like the mountain grass
That cannot but keep the form
Where the mountain hare has lain,
So though one had a lovely face,
And two or three had charm,
Face and charm were in vain.

The poem thus recomposed conforms more closely to the title. It is about memory in general, and particular remembrances are mentioned as supporting illustration, whereas the original is about remembrances in particular and the general nature of memory is mentioned as explanation. The rhetoric is changed but the logical relationship between the propositions remains the same: A *because* B (the original) = B *so* A (the reformulation). In this sense, the two versions can be said to express essentially the same meaning.

They do not, of course, have the same effect. Our rhetorical variant seems clumsy in comparison, awkward in its very conformity. But it has heuristic if not aesthetic value in that it draws attention to features of the original which are lost in the variant. For in the reformulating of the propositional content of the poem, we are necessarily made aware of the logic of its argument.

And it turns out to be very curious, indeed contradictory. If memory is like the mountain grass which cannot do otherwise than retain the impression of the mountain hare, then we would normally conclude that the face and charm associated with people in the past would *not* be in vain since they would be similarly impressed on the memory. Conversely, if they *are* in vain, then we would suppose that this is because they are not remembered, which would be consistent with the mountain grass *not* taking the impression of the mountain hare.

One way of making our revised version consistent with a

normal pattern of reasoning, would be to adjust the first part to accommodate the second. This we could do very simply by omitting *but* in the second line. And, of course, we could regularize the original in just the same way. Alternatively, we might adjust the second part of our variant to accommodate the first. This would require rather more emendation. We might, for example, propose the following:

Memory

Memory is like the mountain grass
That cannot but keep the form
Where the mountain hare has lain,
So the one with a lovely face
And the two or three with charm
Their face and charm retain.

So far, we have been trying to make the argument conform to conventional reasoning while still retaining the semblance of poetic utterance by working within Yeats's prosodic framework. But we could, of course, dispense with the vertical arrangement, the patterns of metre and rhyme, and simply transpose the essentials of the argument into ordinary prosaic terms. The inconsistency I have been referring to is thereby brought out even more starkly:

Memory can be likened to the mountain grass, which will take the impression of the mountain hare that has lain down in it. So the lovely faces of people I have known, and their particular charm, fail to leave an impression on the memory.

But even if we were to normalize the argument (by the simple expedient of deleting *fail to* from the text) the prose paraphrase raises further doubts about its coherence. The mountain grass, for example, may take the impression of the hare, but this is only a trace, a sign of absence, and it is, furthermore, transient, for it does not keep the impression for long. So are we to draw the implication that memory, in like manner, can only provide us with fading traces of past experience? Is that why face and charm are in vain? Again, the mountain grass, it is said, cannot *but* take the form of the resting hare: this seems reasonable since, being inanimate, it is the passive receiver of the impression. Is there an implication, then, that memory is similarly inert, that things impinge upon it, that it cannot be activated to respond, cannot be subject to volition? If so, then the very attempt at remembering is in vain. The prose paraphrase reveals how much of the argument remains inexplicit and in need of explanation.

These reformulations in prose and verse are attempts to recast the propositional content of the original poem to conform to conventional procedures of understanding. What they reveal, I think, is that the meaning of the poem cannot be captured in this way. We need to take another tack. Rather than seeking to adapt the poem to our understanding, we should perhaps try to adapt our understanding to the poem. With this in mind, let us now return to the original, our perceptions of its features now sharpened by contrast with the alternative texts we have been composing.

The difficulties that I have identified arise from the assumption that, given its title, the poem should be read as making reference to human memory in order to describe it, or define it, or explain its effects. As we have seen, measured against customary criteria it is not, as such, very satisfactory. It is unclear and confusing. But what if the poem is not meant to be read referentially in this way? What if we were to read it, not as a *reference* to the nature of memory, but as a *representation* of the very experience of remembering? In this case, the unclarity and inconsequence are entirely appropriate, for these are common features of the experience. Let us then focus on the poem again, but adjusting the lens of our perception to this particular perspective.

We might begin by noticing that the first lines of the poem set it straightaway in a non-referential key. In normal communicative circumstances the pronouns *one* and *two or three* (in the sense of 'a few'—a small but indefinite number) would be used in reference to things, events, persons which are known already and can be identified. If somebody were to say in conversation, for example, that one had a lovely face, then we would naturally want to know, if we did not know already, who or what exactly was being referred to. The pronoun is indexical: it points towards knowledge assumed to be shared. But as the pronouns occur in the poem they point into a void and identify nothing. Who are they, this one, these two or three? They are presumably people, probably women, perhaps young women. We might infer this by invoking usual associations of loveliness and charm. But there is no way of knowing for certain. No identification is provided in the poem, and none is possible by considering any context outside the poem, because no such context exists. The terms fail to refer.[3] What, then, do they do? I suggest that they *represent*. They represent minimal traces of individuals retained in the memory, separate but not easily distinguished, with only the impression of their appearance and manner (face and charm) remaining as vestiges of their identity.

And these images of the past seem to increase in vagueness as the poem proceeds through the first three lines, representing perhaps their gradual fading in memory. All of the images in these first three lines are expressed through indefinite noun phrases, but they diminish in particularity, line by line. Thus we begin with a specific if indefinite person (*one*), go on in the next line to a non-specific number of them (*two or three*), and then to their attributes (*charm* and *face*), now dissociated from the persons concerned and expressed as disembodied abstractions. We might note also that these attributes occur in the third line in the reversed order of their previous mention (*charm and face*, not *face and charm*) which, we might suggest, further strengthens the impression of dissociation. Perception of these effects can perhaps be sharpened by comparing the original with a version rewritten along the following lines:

One had a lovely face,
Another had *lively* charm,
But *their face and charm* were in vain . . .

Here the language no longer represents the experience of remembering: the sense of the elusive fading of images in memory is lost in the increased referential precision.

What, then, of the second part of the poem, the last three lines? If the first three represent the actual working of the mind in the effort of remembering particulars, what do these three lines represent? One might propose that they represent the working of the mind in thinking, in reflecting on the nature of memory in general. But the actual process of thinking does not, of course, have to conform to the canons of logical exposition. It can work by intuitive association, by cognitive scatter, by the metaphorical connection of images. Such a diffuse and divergent process of thinking may not meet the conventional criteria of rational argument, and we would generally seek to edit out its irregularities and inconsistencies, because we seek to record the synoptic result rather than the ruminative process of thinking. But this process has its own reality and carries its own conviction. How, then, is it represented in the second part of the poem?

The most obvious indication that we are moving from the actual to the abstract, from particular instances to generality, is the appearance in line 4 of the logical connector *because*, heralding an explanation. We note, too, that whereas all the noun phrases in the first three lines were indefinite, here in these last three lines they are all definite (*the* mountain grass, *the* form, *the* mountain hare). But although definite, these noun phrases do not make specific reference to particulars assumed to be mutually known (that mountain grass writer and reader both know about, that individual mountain hare they can both identify). They have generic meaning and so express a generalization. These lines, then, have all the appearance of explanation. The assertion in line 3 of the poem is justified by reference to the general truth expressed in the lines which follow. But although these lines have the formal trappings of explanation, in effect, as we have already remarked, they are so vague and contradictory that they explain nothing. On the contrary, they are themselves as inexplicable as the first lines of the poem are inexplicit.

These lines, then, are unsatisfactory as a synoptic record of rational argument. But, as I have already indicated, they do not have to be read in this way. Just as the first three lines can be taken as the representation of the experience of remembering, so these lines can be taken as the representation of the process of reflecting on the experience, not as explanation but rumination. So how might they be interpreted from this point of view?

To begin with we might note that it is not just any grass which takes the impression of any hare: it is the *mountain* grass, the *mountain* hare. Why? The mutual modifier 'mountain' has the effect of bringing the two into close association, and the image of the mountain is made prominent by repetition. What is it about the nature of remembering, then, that is represented by this metaphor? What ideas do the images invoke? One idea might be that as the hare and the grass are of their nature associated, so what is impressed on the mind is something which the mind is already disposed to receive. Another idea might be that since the grass is inanimate and it is the animate hare that acts upon it, so the memory is the passive receiver of impressions and is acted upon in the same way: it cannot but take the impression of something with which it is already associated. This interpretation, based on the association of images, resolves the apparent contradiction in the argument of the poem which was discussed earlier. If we read these lines as ruminative association rather than rational argument, as representation rather than reference, there is no contradiction. And it is just this kind of resolution of disparity by invoking congruences of a different order which gives verbal art, and indeed all art, its essential significance. I shall take up this general point again a little later. But meanwhile there is another idea that is suggested by the images of these particular three lines.

Mountain grass, *mountain* hare. The mental landscape of memory can be likened to mountains. The resemblance is not expounded, simply represented by association, and the reader is left to infer the grounds of the likeness. One might think of the world perceived from a mountain and receding into distance, details becoming indistinct as they do in the memory over time. One might think of the mountain as remote from the surrounding reality as memory is remote from the actuality of experience.

These are some of the ideas that might be invoked by these images. Unconstrained by the usual communicative requirement to shape language to fit contextual conditions or a conventional pattern of accepted sense, the mind is free to exploit the possibilities of meaning:

> The Mind, that Ocean where each kind
> Does streight its own resemblance find;
> Yet it creates, transcending these,
> Far other Worlds and other Seas;
> Annihilating all that's made
> To a green Thought in a green Shade.
> (Andrew Marvell: *The Garden*)

Yet it creates. Destroying an existing order, it brings another one into being. The ideas do not disperse in aimless scatter, but reform into different patterns of meaning consistent with the patterning of the poem. Nothing can be clear and definite. The meaning is bound to be elusive, for the process of rumination, of trying to discover significance, is similarly imprecise, and it is this which, I suggest, is being represented here—the process of understanding, of discovering order, and not the finished product fashioned to conform to conventional standards of rational explanation. T.S. Eliot talks (in *East Coker*) of 'the intolerable wrestle / with words and meanings'. Usually such wrestling is not made public in print. The processes of the mind in its quest for order, the intuitive images, what Wordsworth referred to (in *Tintern Abbey*) as 'gleams of half-extinguished thought', give some intimation of alternative ways of conceiving of the world. But they cannot of their nature be recorded by adherence to convention. They can only be represented. And this, I suggest, is just what poems, like this one by Yeats, seek to do.

Poetry, in this view, in common with all art, necessarily challenges the adequacy of the established order. But this is not to replace it with a competing social orthodoxy, for with poetry there is no fixity. Rather it reveals that there is a reality which conventions cannot of their nature accommodate, in some dimension of meaning between the interstices of what is communal and familiar. For the socially sanctioned ways of using language to describe or expound or explain are not the only ways of using language. The meanings which are encoded to key in with the recurrent contexts of social life are not the only meanings which can be expressed. Once the demands of such contexts are suspended, other meanings, potential within the language, can be released and realigned. Representation, then, as a mode of meaning, is bound to be disruptive and to require a readiness to adopt different ways of reading and thinking for its realization. But in undermining the established and orthodox order of things, poetry sets up an alternative order of its own. For no matter how dispersed its propositional content might be in comparison with what is customary, it is held in place by the prosodic patterning of metre and rhyme. In denying one kind of regularity, the poem asserts its own.

I have argued, then, that the reading of a poem involves the realization of represented meaning. Since this meaning is unstable, elusive of its nature, held in precarious poise within the patterns of verse, it cannot be transposed into other terms, for this would be to reduce it to reference, to the kind of conventional statement that it challenges. It follows, of course, that there can never be any definitive interpretation. I have explored what this Yeats poem means to me, and I have pointed to features of the language which seem to me to give warrant to this meaning. But other interpretations are, of course, possible. We can come to no conclusions. All poems, and indeed all forms of art, contain within their very design the potential for multiple significance. It is precisely because they express realities which cannot be brought within the bounds of social convention that they are relevant.

There are ideas and experience particular to the individual which cannot be made general within the scope of rational description or explanation. Poems represent them, fashion them into a form which we can apprehend without being able to explain.[4]

4 Dissociation from context: the poem on the page

I want now to elaborate a little on the interpretation of representational meaning, and how it is provoked by patterns of language in poems. When discussing the Yeats poem, I made the observation that the indefinite pronoun in the first line (*One* had a lovely face) could not be assigned referential meaning in the normal way because there was nothing in context for it to refer to. This being so, the reader was required to attend to what significance the term might have within the confines of the poem itself. I suggested that the very indefiniteness of the pronoun now became prominent, and could be said to represent the experience of imprecise recollection. The general point here is that the very detachment of a poem from context, its dislocation, so to speak, has the effect of focusing the reader's attention on the language itself and the way it connects with the patterning of language within the poem. The appearance of the poem on a page represents this dislocation; it is set aside, surrounded by white space like a picture frame. And this signals that we are to read it for representational and not referential significance.

With this in mind, let us consider the following piece of language:

> This is just to say that I have eaten the plums that were in the icebox. They were delicious, so sweet and so cold. But you were probably saving them for breakfast. Forgive me.

This is most naturally read as a note, written on a scrap of paper, left in a kitchen for somebody to find in the morning when coming down for breakfast: a little domestic confession and apology, a casual and hasty scribble, whose slightness of import is indicated by the standard opening (This is just to say—no more than that). As such, its purpose would be served just as well by an alternative phrasing:

This is just to say that I found some plums in the icebox. They were so deliciously sweet and cold that I ate them all. But then I realized that you were probably saving them for breakfast. Sorry about that. See you later.

The recipient of such a note, a wife, let us suppose, or some significant other, knowing who the note was from and seeing it in the familiar context of her kitchen, would in all likelihood glance at it briefly, take in the gist, react with exasperation, perhaps, or tolerant forebearance, and think no more about it. It would be strange if she were to subject the language to close scrutiny and look for any special significance in the choice of word or phrase. It is, after all, only a note. As such it connects up with a familiar context and is part of the continuity of domestic life. There is no more reason for paying particular attention to its language than there would be for pondering on the appearance of the crockery or the colour of the curtains.

But it happens that the propositions expressed in this note have actually been dislocated and fashioned into a poem. It runs as follows:

This Is Just to Say

I have eaten
the plums
that were in
the icebox

and which
you were probably
saving
for breakfast

Forgive me
they were delicious
so sweet
and so cold
(William Carlos Williams)[5]

This is no longer a note. The propositions make no reference to any shared knowledge of plums or icebox: they are displayed as significant in themselves without connection with context, disposed in a pattern that lays claim to its own independent coherence. And we are provoked into closer scrutiny, seeking to discern why the apparently trivial content of an informal note should be offered to us as being in some way noteworthy.

One consequence of this contextual detachment is that we are positioned differently as readers. In the case of the note we are in the position of a third-person observer of other people's private communication which has point only for them, and which we have no business to read even if we thought it of any interest to do so. In the case of the poem, on the other hand, we are drawn into engagement. The supposed participants and the context they appear to share are incorporated into a text which has been composed and made public by somebody else, a superordinate first-person writer, and open to interpretation by a superordinate second-person reader. The people who are involved as participants in the note take on third-person status in the poem, and, in consequence, the reader shifts from observer to participant role.

In this role, the reader is called upon to interpret what is expressed. This cannot be done by usual referential means, for this depends on contextual location, but only by a consideration of what the language enclosed within the poem might represent. What, then, might it represent?

We might notice, to begin with, that the expression 'Forgive me' is made prominent by the only appearance in the text of a capital letter, its occurrence at the beginning of the verse, and by the fact that it is the only time up to this point in the poem that a complete sentence is enclosed within a single line. All the other lines are linked together in a syntactic continuity, but this one stands structurally independent. Once our attention is focused in this way, we might further notice that the expression itself seems to be rather formal, and one which we might normally associate with actions rather more reprehensible than the eating of plums. The first person, the 'I' of the poem, has taken his pleasure (let us suppose that this first person is male) by depriving the second person 'you' of the poem of something she (let us suppose) has been saving. This word 'saving' is also given prominence, for it is the only word in the poem which has a line to itself. What implications or images are called to mind by such emphasis? Saving, keeping carefully, preserving. Could it be that the eating of the plums represents the tasting of forbidden fruit, and the deprivation of (in Andrew Marvell's phrase) a 'long preserved virginity'. Perhaps. At all events, whatever the experience, the first person here emphasizes his pleasure rather than his guilt, for this too is made prominent by being expressed as a complete sentence within a single line: 'they were delicious'. And this seems odd. One normally associates confession with contrition. One would expect an apology to be followed by an expression of regret at committing the act in question. But here, on the contrary, what is expressed is not regret but relish. It is as if this first person is suggesting that the pleasure of the experience is itself a reason for forgiveness.

But the pleasure is itself somewhat ambivalent. The last two lines of the poem provide a gloss on the one preceding and explain why the plums were delicious (they were sweet and cold). But whereas, as we have already noted, all the other lines of the poem consist of syntactic elements which are combined in sequential structure, these last two lines consist of elements which are structurally in parallel: they do not combine, they co-occur. They arrest the syntactic movement of the poem and give it closure with assertive emphasis, rather like two chords completing the movement of a musical composition. This formal closure seems to imply a conclusion of some kind and the repetition suggests the insistence on a particular point. The point has to do with contrast, signalled by the conjunction and the repeated word *so*: 'so sweet and [yet] so cold'. One might compare the common phrase 'so near and (yet) so far' (as opposed to 'so near and far'). If there were no such repetition, then the contrastive effect would lose its force. Consider, for example, this remark by Lear to Cordelia and her reply:

LEAR   So young, and so untender?
CORDELIA   So young, my lord, and true.

In the concluding chords of these last lines, then, the final note is one of coldness.

As we focus on the particular way in which the propositional content of the poem is formulated, we begin to discern the possibilities of an undercurrent of implied significance. The eating of the plums, apparently so trivial an act in itself, can be read as representing the experience of a human relationship and an ambivalent attitude towards it: in part guilt, in part gratification; in part positive and pleasurable, in part negative and alienating. This further significance is faint, subjectively apprehended, inexplicit and elusive, as all represented meanings must be, but it is only in the discerning of meanings of this kind in the patterning of language that the point of the poem can be realized.

And of course, the process of interpreting that the poem provokes us into in effect denies the implication of its title. This, the
poem as distinct from the note, is *not* just to say that he has eaten
the plums in the icebox. It is to say more than that, and it is in the
manner of the saying that this other dimension of meaning is
represented. It follows that if the manner of saying were to be
altered, then the meanings that I have been reading into this one
would no longer have the same warrant in the text. Consider, for
example, the effects of the following reformulation:

This Is Just to Say

I have eaten the plums
that were in
the icebox

they were
delicious
so cold
and sweet

I'm sorry
you were probably
saving them
for breakfast

Since this is presented as a poem, we would be drawn into a quest
for representational significance as before, but we would be
induced to read different meanings into it. This text constitutes a
different interpretative occasion. And to place this version alongside the original enables us to see more clearly what is distinctive
about each, and the extent to which different interpretations seem
to be warranted by the linguistic features of the texts. One might
then consider relating these to other variants, composed by mod-
ifying the content more freely, but conforming more closely to traditional poetic convention, to see what different interpretations
they might invoke. One might propose the following:

I found the plums that you were keeping
In the icebox cold and sweet,
I ate them all while you were sleeping.
Forgive me. They were good to eat.

Or something more jaunty, to illustrate the point made earlier that poetry should be not protected by reverence:

> Forgive me, I've been rather hasty.
> I ate your plums, and they were tasty.

Later in this book I shall be looking at ways in which alternative versions of this kind might be put to pedagogic use, but for the present they can serve to draw attention to another feature of the original poem. This is that it is markedly free of the verbal devices which are traditionally associated with poetry: there are no tropes and figures, no alliteration, no metrical regularity or rhyme. It is indeed as if there is a deliberate avoidance of obvious artifice, as if we are being provoked into finding something remarkable in the unremarkable events of everyday life. So quite apart from any particular significance that might be attached to the eating of the plums, what seems to be suggested here, more generally, is the way in which commonplace occurrences and common language can be transposed into a different key. In this respect, what the poem represents is the transfiguration of the trivial. I have indicated a musical analogy in my discussion of this poem. There is here a parallel with painting also. A casual note is taken out of its kitchen context and fashioned into a poem on a page, rather as items of crockery, a dish of plums indeed, might be similarly dislocated from their surroundings and painted on a canvas as still life.

5 Verbal patterning and the grammar of representation

The dissociation of language from its normal connections with context, further confirmed by the way it is fashioned into prosodic shape, directs the attention of the reader to the language itself enclosed within the confines of the poem. Interpretation is the function of a heightened awareness of how language can mean, how its resources can be exploited to express different perspectives on familiar reality. In this respect, the reading of a poem is itself the representation of a renewal of our experience of the language, freed from the usual dulling effect of context. For it is common communicative practice to use language only as a convenient means for identifying relevant contextual information. Once the identification is made, once an expression effectively refers us to something and so acts indexically to point out some feature of the familiar world, then it can be said to have discharged its purpose in this case and we need pay no further heed to it. This is not a matter for regret. We could not use language effectively in the transaction of everyday business if we did not treat it in this fashion. It would not do for us to subject every use of language to close scrutiny and pass under review all the possible meanings it might signify. To do this would be to deny the co-operative principle upon which effective communication depends.[6] So the normal referential function of language necessarily deflects attention from the language itself. There are, of course, other uses of language apart from the directly referential that I have outlined here, but for the moment I want to make a clear, if somewhat simplistic, comparison between the referential mode of meaning which characterizes everyday transactions, and the representational mode which, I have been arguing, is distinctive of poetic utterance. Actually, I believe it is distinctive of literature in general, but it is the verbal art of lyric poetry which is my particular concern in this book.

The essential point about representation, as I have defined it, is that it is the use of language to create its own conditions of relevance. Whereas with reference language is dependent on external and actual context, with representation, context is internal, potential, and dependent on language: it takes shape in the verbal patterns of the poem. These, as I have tried to demonstrate, provoke the reader into divergent interpretation, that is to say, into the assembling of contexts which make sense. What these patterns do is to exploit the latent possibilities of language and in discerning them the reader is made aware of a realignment of established categories of meaning. I want now to consider more closely how this is done, focusing specifically on features of grammar.

I shall take as my text some simple lines by Wordsworth. Their very simplicity is a challenge, for on the face of it, they appear to be remarkable only for their banality. The circumstances of their composition and a description of the scene that inspired them appear in the journal of his sister Dorothy as follows:

> When I returned, I found William writing a poem descriptive of the sights and sounds we saw and heard. There was the gentle flowing of the stream, the glittering lively lake, green fields without a living creature to be seen on them, behind us, a flat pasture with 42 cattle feeding; to our left, the road leading to the hamlet, no smoke there, the sun shining on the bare roofs. The people were at work ploughing, harrowing and sowing; lasses spreading dung, a dog's barking now and then, cocks crowing, birds twittering, the snow in patches on the top of the highest hills, yellow palms, purple and green twigs on the birches, ashes with their glittering spikes quite bare. The hawthorn a bright green, with black stems under the oak. The moss of the oak glossy . . . William finished his poem before we got to the foot of Kirkstone.
>
> (Dorothy Wordsworth: *Journal, April 16, 1802*)

And here is William's poem:

The Cock is crowing,
The stream is flowing,
The small birds twitter,
The lake doth glitter,
The green field sleeps in the sun;
The oldest and youngest
Are at work with the strongest;
The cattle are grazing;
Their heads never raising;
There are forty feeding like one!

Like an army defeated
The snow hath retreated,
And now doth fare ill
On the top of the bare hill:
The Ploughboy is whooping—anon—anon: ¯
There's joy in the mountains;
There's life in the fountains;
Small clouds are sailing,
Blue sky prevailing;
The rain is over and gone!

Now I do not suppose that anyone would wish to make any great aesthetic claims for this poem. Indeed, we might be tempted to dismiss it as doggerel—Wordsworth on one of his (not infrequent) off-days. And yet, as with the graveyard verses we started with, it raises interesting questions, particularly in comparison with his sister's referential version. What, for example, motivates his selection of the sights and sounds they have both seen, and what do we make of the way he has expressed and arranged them in his poem? How are they *represented*?

To begin with the obvious, Dorothy refers to a good deal of detail which William disregards. The different kinds of human activity which she notes (ploughing, harrowing, sowing, dung-spreading) are generalized into the phrase 'at work'. The closely observed features of the trees, the purple and green twigs of the birch, the glittering spikes of the ash, the green and black hawthorn, the glossy oak, all disappear. In William's poem there is no tree in sight. Indeed, what he has to offer in the way of description is spare in the extreme, almost perversely so, as if to provoke the charge of triviality. The first five lines of the poem are a list of items expressed in the simplest of syntax and contained within rudimentary patterns of verse form. Of the twenty or so noun phrases in the two verses (on average about one per line) only five are garnished with descriptive adjectives and even these are very meagre and uninspiring (*small* birds, *green* field, *bare* hill, *small* clouds, *blue* sky—blue sky, I ask you!) And yet, composed into a poem as they are, these sparse observations are offered to us as if they were significant. But significant of what?

The absence of elaboration and adornment can be read as deliberate avoidance and to suggest, therefore, that what is represented here is a perception of what is essential about the scene, some elemental and simple symmetry which underlies all the scattered and incidental detail of surface impression which Dorothy records in her account. With this possibility in mind, we might now subject the language of the poem to closer scrutiny.

Consider the first four lines. They constitute, at one level at least, a very clear and obvious design. Each line consists of the same self-contained syntactic structure: noun phrase and verb phrase, subject and intransitive verb. The structural equivalence is further confirmed by the recurrence of the definite article at the beginning of each line. This is almost like an exercise in pattern practice. Within this design, the first two lines combine into a unit with their equivalent present continuous verb forms and feminine rhymes (*crowing* and *flowing*); and this is nicely balanced against the unit of the second two lines with their recurrent simple present verb forms and their different, but also feminine, rhymes (*twitter* and *glitter*).

But if we now consider the subject noun phrases of the sentences in these first four lines a rather different pattern emerges. All the lines are marked as alike by the recurrence of the initial definite article. But it is clear that semantically line 1 relates to line 3, in that in both cases the nouns are animate; and, furthermore, both denote birds (*cock* and *birds*). It is equally clear that line 2 is linked to line 4 in that both nouns are inanimate; and, furthermore, both denote stretches of water (*stream* and *lake*).

On the one hand, then, we can identify a pattern which relates lines 1 and 2, 3 and 4 by virtue of the equivalence of tense and aspect marking on the verb; and on the other hand we can identify a pattern which relates lines 1 and 3, 2 and 4 by virtue of the equivalence of animacy/inanimacy of the noun. What are we to make of this?

Animacy, tense, and aspect are, of course, semantico-grammatical categories which encode concepts of reality, and record the way we normally perceive the nature of existence. Thus, with respect to animacy, things are either living and sentient beings (like birds) or non-living objects (like streams). Tense and aspect categories are more complex. Events are thought of: either as extending continuously over a period of time in the present (*is flowing*) or in the past (*was flowing*); or as occurring at a point in time, present or past (*twitter, twittered*). Kinds of temporal experience are, then, encoded in English by the following semantic co-ordinates:

	point in time	*period of time*
present	present simple	present continuous
past	past simple	past continuous

This chart is not, of course, complete (for one thing, there is no mention of the perfective aspect), but it will serve for our present purposes.

Returning, then, to the two different patterns we have identified in the opening four lines of Wordsworth's poem, we can see that in the first of them (comprising lines 1 and 2, lines 3 and 4), there is a fusion of the normally distinct concepts of animacy/inanimacy; and in the second of them (comprising lines 1 and 3, lines 2 and 4), a fusion of the normally distinct concepts of period of time and point in time. If we now superimpose one pattern on the other, we arrive at a convergence of contrary perceptions, made coherent in the structural and prosodic regularities of the verse form. In consequence what we can read the poem as representing is a scene in which, at a level of essential being below superficial appearances, animate creatures and inanimate objects partake of the same mode of existence, and in which time is experienced as both momentary and continuous, as both state and process.

We should note too that this experience is prosodically contained within the lines of verse. For each of these first four lines expresses within itself a different process, and yet their metrical and grammatical equivalence and their vertical arrangement suggests repetition and sameness. They suggest that all difference is reduced to generality, all movement held in stasis. In the representation of the experience, the actual shape of the poem plays its part. I shall have more to say on the significance of the linear arrangement of poetry a little later (in Chapter 8).

We might propose, then, that the objects and events of the scene that Dorothy describes are reduced to their elemental essentials and so ordered into patterns of language in the poem as to represent the unifying vision of an alternative order of existence, one which admits of no other means of expression. The language is elementary because it represents what is elemental. This Wordsworthian vision of the sentience of all nature and of a reality which is continuous within particular moments in time is one which finds fuller and more impressive expression in other poems, but it can be discerned here too in the use of language in this rather more rudimentary poetic sketch. The vision is, of its nature, elusive and fleeting (as Wordsworth himself knew only too well). And this too is represented here. For the patterning of language I have been discussing, so completely symmetrical in the first two lines, becomes less regular in the two that follow. The fifth line:

The green field sleeps in the sun;

while confirming the fusion of animacy and inanimacy and of different perspectives on time, introduces a variation which in effect rearranges the preceding lines into a larger verbal design, which in its turn will have implications for the interpretation of the poem as a whole. But such interpretation I shall leave for readers themselves to engage in (should they feel inclined). My purpose at present is to use the poem to illustrate the representational use of language in poetry in general, to demonstrate how established concepts encoded in linguistic categories can be realigned to represent reality in a new dimension.

This representation is inherent in the verbal patterns. As we have already seen with other poems, if the patterns change, then the representation changes accordingly. So if we were to select and order the details of Dorothy's referential description in a different way, then the effects that I have been reading into William's poem would no longer be warranted. We would look for others. It might be of interest, for example, (following the precedence of our discussion in previous chapters) to compare the original with an alternative selection and ordering along these lines:

The cocks are crowing,
The gentle stream is flowing,
The birds are twittering,
The lively lake is glittering,
On the hills there is snow to be seen;
People are harrowing,
Ploughing and sowing,
The oak tree is mossy,
The hawthorn is glossy,
The birch twigs are purple and green.

As I have already indicated, there are pedagogic possibilities in this derivation of variants, and these I shall be looking into later in the book. But for the moment I want to continue my enquiry into the poetic exploitation of grammar. This time I shall take my text from Wordworth's friend and fellow poet, Samuel Taylor Coleridge.

6 Time and place in a different dimension

In the case of the Wordsworth poem, the relevant co-ordinates displayed in the table on page 36 were those of aspect (period of time/point in time). I want now to consider a case where those of tense (present/past) come into play. The text this time is Coleridge's poem *The Rime of the Ancient Mariner*, and in particular the opening verses. I want to enquire into how the simple tenses of English are used at the beginning of the poem to create an appropriate setting for the mariner and the tale he has to tell.

The mariner makes his appearance in the very first line of the poem:

> It is an ancient Mariner,
> And he stoppeth one of three . . .

Right from the start, we might note, he has something of an air of mystery about him: for the grammar of this first line makes him appear suddenly out of nowhere. The pronoun 'it' in conventional referential use is either deictic, and so presupposes presence, or anaphoric, and so presupposes previous mention. Either way, known pre-existence is assumed. So the structure 'It is . . . (+ noun phrase)' would normally be used to identify someone (or something) known to the speaker and in response to a request for information, as, for example:

A: Who is that person over there?
B: It is an ancient mariner. Let me introduce you.

The question provides a context in that it refers to some pre-existing state of affairs. But in the poem there is no question to respond to, no preceding context, no previous existence. The mariner just appears out of the blue: an apparition, indeed, rather than an appearance. We can perhaps best demonstrate this by (as before) comparing the original with alternative versions. Consider the difference in effect if the opening lines had run like this, for example:

> There was once an ancient mariner
> And he stopped one of three ...

> An ancient mariner one day
> Came by, stopped one of three ...

These variants also differ from the original version (it will have been noticed) in that the tense has been changed from the simple present to the simple past. And here we come to the main theme of this chapter. For the mystery of the mariner's abrupt appearance is sustained by an idiosyncratic use of tense.

Coleridge's mariner appears in the present. His presence is invoked, here and now, before our very eyes. But in spite of the use of the simple present, he is not simply in the present. For the events in these opening lines of the poem are represented as taking place in the past as well. The mariner's existence and his encounter with the wedding-guest (the one of three) would seem to belong simultaneously to two quite separate temporal worlds. He inhabits a (referentially) impossible space in time defined by incompatible dimensions. Thus, as we have already noted, in the first two lines he appears in the present and accosts the wedding-guest in the present. Then follows the wedding-guest's perplexed expostulation, recorded in direct speech:

> It is an ancient Mariner,
> And he stoppeth one of three.
> 'By thy long grey beard and glittering eye,
> Now wherefore stopp'st thou me?

> The Bridegroom's doors are opened wide,
> And I am next of kin;
> The guests are met, the feast is set:
> May'st hear the merry din.'

The next three verses then show no less than seven shifts of tense, backwards and forwards, from simple present to simple past:

> He *holds* him with his skinny hand,   PRESENT
> 'There was a ship,' *quoth* he.   PAST

'Hold off! unhand me, grey-beard loon!'
Eftsoons his hand *dropt* he.   PAST

He *holds* him with his glittering eye—   PRESENT
The Wedding-Guest *stood* still,   PAST
And *listens* like a three years' child: PRESENT
The Mariner *hath* his will.   PRESENT

The Wedding-Guest *sat* on a stone: PAST
He *cannot* choose but hear;   PRESENT
And thus *spake* on that ancient man,   PAST
The bright-eyed Mariner.

The mariner holds the wedding-guest with his skinny hand in the
present, but releases his hold in the past; only to hold him again,
with his eye this time, in the present. The wedding-guest stands
still and sits down in the past but manages to listen to the mariner
in the present, although the mariner speaks to him in the past. It is
all very bewildering. What, we might wonder, is going on here?
What reason could there be for all this shuttlecock shifting of
tense?

One explanation might be, of course, that there is no reason at
all. Perhaps Coleridge was simply careless and did not do his
proof-reading properly, and in the act of composition simply
selected verb forms at random, treating the tenses as if they were
in free variation. Perhaps. But the common referential convention
is to be consistent, so one would expect indifference to lead to
conformity of tense usage rather than this complex variation. It
should be noted, too, that in all cases the tenses could be altered
into regularity without affecting either rhythm or rhyme, so Coleridge is not constrained by the exigencies of verse composition. So
if these shifts are not required by rhyme, by what reason are they
required? The fact is that they are there in the text of the poem,
and as has been repeatedly argued in this book (and as Coleridge
would himself recognize) *everything* in a poetic text carries an implication of relevance. Assuming, then, that this alternation of
tense is to be read as significant, what is it significant *of*? In referential terms it is contradictory. Can it be coherently understood
as representation?[7]

At this point we need to elaborate a little on our previous discussion about what the tenses in English normally signify. As we
have already noted, the simple present relates to point in time. It is

naturally used, therefore, to specify an event which occurs at the moment of speaking and so is within the same framework of time and space as the speaker. This was the use that was identified in Wordsworth's line:

The small birds twitter.

Here the event and the experience of the event are co-occurrent, both of them immediate to the moment, here and now. But this tense can also denote a recurrence of events displaced from immediate context and generalized. Thus the expression:

Small birds twitter.

might be used to describe particular birds now and actual in the immediate vicinity, or it could be used to make a statement about the behaviour of small birds in general (it is of the nature of small birds to twitter). So this tense can on the one hand denote particular perceptions of actual events which are immediate to the experience of here and now, *contextually* present, and on the other hand it can denote generalized events, not directly perceived at the moment but *conceptually* present as an abstract proposition. So we can think of this tense as expressing experience of events along a scale from the perception of actual instances, the immediacy of here and now, at one end, to the conception of abstract generalities at the other.

What, then, of the simple past? This, of course, signifies a detachment from shared space and time. It expresses the there and then of events remote from the immediacy of direct perception. But as with the simple present, the events can either be perceived as particular and actual, or conceived as abstracted into generality. We might compare:

She worked until five last Friday.
She worked until five on Fridays.

The first of these expressions has to do with a single event, localized in time, and contextualized as a particular occurrence. The second has to do with a plurality of events, conceptualized as general recurrence. This second meaning (but not the first) can be more explicitly signalled by the auxiliary *used to*. The following, therefore, are semantically equivalent:

She worked until five on Fridays.
She used to work until five on Fridays.

But we cannot have:

She used to work until five last Friday.

The standard semantic meanings of these simple tenses in English, then, can be plotted along two parameters: past/present on the one hand, and degrees of generality on the other. In the first case, the meaning is morphologically marked on the verb (*works/ worked*). In the second case, whether an event is more or less general (conceptually abstract), or more or less particular (contextually actual) is not signalled by the verb form itself but by the company it keeps with other constituents (*Small birds twitter* vs. *The small birds twitter; She worked* on **Fridays** vs. *She worked last Friday*).

With these semantic observations in mind, we can now return to the opening lines of Coleridge's poem. The alternation of the two simple tenses can be read as representing an alternation between different perspectives on time. One of these has, obviously, to do with the past/present parameter, the temporal *location* of events. The mariner is, mysteriously, both here and now, and there and then, inhabiting a world in which past and present are fused and unified in some time/space dimension that defies explanation. The other perspective has to do with the second parameter that was mentioned, with the *nature* of the events. These are in a sense particular, but since they cannot of their nature be referred to (for they cannot be contextually located outside the poem), they cannot really be actual. The company the verb forms keep here makes them ambiguous. They represent events which are particular, and by implication actual, yet abstract too, and so by implication general.

The kind of reality which the ancient mariner carries with him, and creates by his presence, is projected by the use of simple tenses like frames in a film, with close-up and distance shots providing different perspectives on the 'same' event. The mariner is indeed a strange and ghost-like apparition: actual and existing in both present and past time, here and now, there and then, here and then, there and now. And yet, because of such contradictions, he is abstract too, with no particular existence in time and place at all. His mode of being (it is of some interest to note) resembles that of God as apprehended by Professor Godbole in E.M. Forster's novel *A Passage to India*:

. . . Professor Godbole stands in the presence of God. God is not born yet—that will occur at midnight—but He has also been born centuries ago, nor can He ever be born, because He is the Lord of the Universe, who transcends human processes. He is, was not, is not, was. He and Professor Godbole stood at opposite ends of the same strip of carpet.

Notice that Professor Godbole both *stands* in the presence of God and *stood* on the same strip of carpet, just as the wedding-guest both *listens* to the ancient mariner and *stood* still at the same time and in the same place. And in both cases, the time and place are also timeless and without location. Such an ambivalent and mysterious world is proper habitation for the ancient mariner. For his being is the very life-in-death which his tale describes as he passes 'like night, from land to land'. Here the conceptual categories encoded in language which we use to divide up reality have no validity. And the voyage of the ship, the killing of the albatross, the sight of the water snakes, though all perceived and described as particular events, are also momentous in their general and abstract significance. Thus contradictions are reconciled, and aspects of reality realigned, in this world which can have no referential stability in truth, but which carries its own elusive conviction by the manner of its representation through specific uses of language.

7 Other patterns, alternative realities

In the last two chapters I have been looking at examples of how the grammatical categories of tense and aspect are realigned to provoke the reading of poetry as representation. But this manipulation is not, of course, confined to such categories, nor to this level of language. The principle of realignment or reassembly of linguistic encodings in poetry operates across all levels. As far as the phonological and lexical levels are concerned, the principle has traditionally been given recognition in the description of alliteration, assonance, metre, and rhyme on the one hand, and of metaphor on the other. The point I would wish to make here is that although these features are distinguishable by their level of operation, they all have a common representational function, which in particular instances they combine to discharge. It is this, I would argue, that we need to realize in interpretation. In other words, what we need to do is to consider how phonological, lexical, and grammatical realignments pattern together to representational effect. I have already suggested how this congruence works in the little Wordsworth poem considered earlier, with the variations in aspect keying in with the simplicity of lexical choice, syntactic structure, and metrical movement. I want now to consider two more examples of how alignments at different levels are worked into a combined and coherent pattern. Both of them deal with the experience of time so in that respect they continue the theme of the poems by Wordsworth and Coleridge we have just been considering.

The first is an extract from a poem by Alexander Pope entitled *An Epistle to Miss Blount, on her leaving the Town after the Coronation*. It is about a young woman of fashion in the early eighteenth century who has been obliged to leave town to spend some time in the country.

> She went from Op'ra, Park, Assembly, Play,
> To morning walks, and pray'rs three hours a day;
> To part her time 'twixt reading and bohea,
> To muse, and spill her solitary tea,
> Or o'er cold coffee trifle with the spoon,
> Count the slow clock, and dine exact at noon ...

Consider, to begin with, how the patterning of sound in the first line expresses the liveliness of the entertainments of the town. The metrical tempo is appropriately sprightly: the stressed syllables, reinforced by the voiced plosive consonants (*Op'ra, Park, Play*), beat out a sequence of crowded events. And these events are expressed as a lexical list of abstract nouns (*Op'ra, Play*, not **an** *op'ra*, **a** *play*, or *operas* and *plays* in the plural) which is of itself perhaps suggestive of a breathless round of indiscriminate pleasure: no sooner is one type of entertainment over than the next begins, with no time to appreciate the difference. And yet, although this lexical listing suggests a sameness, there are phonological indications of variety, for the letter *a* in these four words corresponds with different sound values (ɒprə, pɑːk, əsemblɪ, pleɪ).

The second line, which completes the couplet, is in marked contrast. Here the tempo slows right down, drawn out by the long vowels (*morning, walks, prayers, hours*), so that events are represented as elongated and dreary. Time which tripped so rapidly before now drags its feet. Whereas the events in town were all crowded feverishly into one line, these two country events, dull in themselves, the nouns which describe them heavy with modification (**morning** *walks*, *pray'rs* **three hours a day**), now struggle to fill the same space.

Consider the fifth line. The trifling with the spoon, the cold coffee are, one might suggest, the lexical signals of lassitude. This is reinforced by the repetition of sound in the first two syllables of the line (*or o'er*), which is the onomatopoeic representation of a yawn. And this comes, significantly enough, after three lines which, in describing the dull repetition of routine, all begin with the same word (*To*), whose equivalent position in the line diminishes the difference of grammatical function.

Or take the last line. Here tedium is described by the expressions *slow clock* and *dine exact at noon* but the description is again enhanced by the sound patterns. Every word but one in this line is monosyllabic and six of them carry stress. The monosyllables spell out monotony. The line has a beat which represents the counting out of moments of time in the slow course of a tedious day.

The point, then, is that the experience of this young lady exiled in the country is expressed in the verbal patterns of the verse which are fashioned out of the congruent realignments of language at different levels: phonological, lexical, grammatical. To discover these patterns is to find grounds for interpretation. To change the patterns is to change the interpretative possibilities. Thus the following variants on these lines by Pope would have different (and I would suggest diminished) representational effects:

> She went from evenings at a ball or play
> To stables, churches, walks and prayers each day;
> Parting her time 'twixt reading and bohea,
> Taking her time to drink her lonely tea,
> Trifling over coffee with her spoon,
> Counting each minute, dining just at noon.

My second example is a translation from the Chinese of two lines:

> Swiftly the years, beyond recall.
> Solemn the stillness of this Spring morning.[8]

The first thing to note here is that each of these lines has the appearance of a sentence. The fact that each one begins with a capital letter is not decisive, of course, since this is customary in verse. But each one also ends with a full stop, and this would usually mark sentential closure. But these lines are, grammatically speaking, not sentences at all. A crucial element is missing, namely the finite verb. As we have already noted in previous discussion, it is the finite verb which signifies the temporal location and nature of events. In referential terms, therefore, there is no specification of time in these lines. The propositions expressed are incomplete: since they are grammatically non-finite, their meaning is infinite. But although no time can be referred to in these lines, it can be represented, and this is done by the patterning in of lexis with grammatical categories other than those of the verb.

There are two noun phrases which express time, one in each line. One of these, *the years*, expresses a long period of time, and the other, *this Spring morning*, a brief one, which, by virtue of the demonstrative determiner *this*, is located in the immediate present. But it is also associated with another period of time, namely the season of Spring. So in these lines we have three periods of time in decreasing size: year, season, morning. Notice, now, that the period of time in line 1 keeps company with adverbial phrases (*swiftly* and *beyond recall*). Although adverbs are a notoriously complex category, they can (as their name implies) be generally associated with the verb phrase and so are bound up with the notion of process. The short period of time in line 2, on the other hand, keeps company with adjective and noun expressions (*solemn*, *stillness*) and these parts of speech are generally bound up with the notion of state rather than process.

These combinations of lexical item and part of speech category represent time in the first line as a continuing process over a long period, apart from present perception, and indeed beyond recall, and in the second line as a state over a brief period, here and now in the present, as indicated by the determiner, but only fleetingly so, not fixed in finiteness. The effect is of the stillness of the morning held temporarily in suspense from time in a moment of elusive stability. The dynamic process of time through the years, and the static immediate moment of the spring morning coexist on the same plane of infinity, in a different dimension from that which we can refer to conventionally by tense and aspect marking on the finite verb.

Again, we can bring out the significance of the verbal patterning of the original by comparing it with rephrased variants. We could, for example, provide finite verbs and alter the structures in certain ways:

Swift are the years, beyond recall.
Solemn and still is this Spring morning.

The years are swift, beyond recall.
This Spring morning is solemn and still.

We might, more ambitiously, expand the original by rendering an interpretation into an alternative poem. For example:

The years run swiftly on, their past
Fades to a distant time, and all
The present moments are the last,
As years recede, beyond recall.

And yet the stillness of this day
Holds all time, motionless, to bring
A sense of present things that stay
And solemnize this morning Spring.

This version, cast in conventional poetic idiom, brings out a further feature of the original lines. The very fact that each consists of a set of phrases syntactically unconnected within each line and across lines means that the images they express cannot be combined but only associated. The two lines, appearing in parallel, suggest not sequence but simultaneity: one image of time is superimposed on the other. The vertical juxtaposition itself, the physical alignment of the lines, keys in with the way the experience of time is represented by lexical and grammatical means. I have already touched on the significance of the vertical arrangement of poetic language (in Chapters 2 and 5) and I want now to consider it more closely.

8 Parallel lines and parallel texts

I made the point earlier (in Chapter 3) that, given the way poetic language is fashioned into vertical array, one should not expect that poems should be interpretable by applying the conventions of rationality. These are, after all, based essentially on the principle of *combination*. Their very parallel patterning precludes poems from being arguments in the normal sense. Thus I suggested that what was expressed in the Yeats poem was not the end product of thinking, but rather the process of thinking itself, the experience of exploring ideas beyond the charted limits of logic and common sense. But just as we should not expect poems to be consequential in argument, so we should not expect them either to be sequential in description. For again, as we saw with the Wordsworth poem in Chapter 5, what they represent is a dimension of awareness which cannot of its nature be accommodated within conventional norms, and this dimension is physically displayed by the vertical arrangement of lines. As I indicated earlier, the substantial shape of a poem is part of its significance.

As further illustration of this, I want to look at a poem which takes us back to the graveyard theme we began with, and which also links up with the preceding discussion about the representation of time. I refer to Gray's *Elegy written in a Country Churchyard*. The opening verse runs as follows:

> The curfew tolls the knell of parting day,
> The lowing herd winds slowly o'er the lea,
> The ploughman homeward plods his weary way,
> And leaves the world to darkness and to me.

Here (as with the poem by Wordsworth we considered earlier) we have the description of a scene. It seems at first sight straightforward enough: we have first the sound of the curfew, then the lowing herd, then the ploughman. The question arises though as to whether these features of the scene are co-occurrent or consecutive. In one sense, of course, they are consecutive because this is their order of appearance in the poem as we read it. But, as was pointed out earlier (in Chapter 3), poems are designed to provoke repeated reading, and to overcome the limitations of linearity. Thus, the features of the description are not set down end to end in a continuous string, as would be the case with prose, but they are assembled in lines one on top of the other in a vertical column. The end of each line marks a closure, both metrically and grammatically, and so there is discontinuity between them. We return to our point of departure at the beginning of the next line. In this respect, we read each line, therefore, as a separate unit of meaning, associated as parts of a vertical pattern but not horizontally combined. The regularity of the metre measures off each line in complete and equivalent prosodic units enclosing complete and equivalent syntactic structures and this, together with the pattern of the rhyme scheme, which necessarily links later lines with earlier ones, all conspires to convey an impression of co-occurrence and arrested movement.

The scene is composed in two dimensions rather than one, in a pictorial rather than a normal linguistic mode. And as with a picture, what is described is held in suspended animation. There is movement within the individual propositional images (the herd making its way over the meadow, the ploughman plodding home) but the movement is arrested in a sort of stasis as these temporal events are transposed into a spatial pattern whereby each of the images (aural in the first line, visual in the other two) make, as it were, a simultaneous appearance on the scene. Furthermore, appearing as they do as equivalent elements in the composition of the verse, being in parallel and cut to the same metrical shape, the events that are perceived are represented, for all their propositional differences, as in some sense the same. The vertical array of the lines of the poem projects a composition after the manner of painting, but by virtue of the prosodic patterns into which they fit, the lines also become variations on a theme after the manner of music. They appeal to both visual and aural senses. They constitute a kind of fusion of pictorial composition and musical arrangement.

Now this prosodic shape of the verse has its effects on the propositions that are expressed within it. Figuring as they do as parts of a pattern, the events described already take on something of an abstract quality, and this is reinforced by the congruent way in which language is used for their description. It is here that we make contact again with the observations made earlier about the exploitation of linguistic resources to represent different perceptions of time.

The verb form which is used in these opening lines of the *Elegy* is the simple present. As we have seen, this tense can signify either an actual and particular event occurring at the time of speech, or events in the abstract, generalizations from particular instances. The same distinction attaches to the definite article: it can be used contextually to make a definite reference to something specific and identifiable, or it can be used conceptually to make generic reference to a class of things in the abstract. How, then, are tense and article used in these lines: to describe particular events or abstract generalities?

The answer is both, and neither. We cannot as readers ratify the use of the definite article as a way of pointing out something particular assumed to be mutually identifiable—the ploughman, *you* know, the ploughman over there, the ploughman we have been talking about—because we have no common context of reference. In this respect, the ploughman is a generic abstraction. Similarly, we cannot identify any particular lowing herd winding over the lea, because we are not there. But again, in a sense, we *are* there, and the herd and the ploughman figure as particular images, for a mutual context is brought about by the very use of the definite article, since this of its nature carries the supposition of shared experience. And in association with the present simple tense, it draws us into the immediacy of the moment, and creates the illusion of presence.

The description of the scene fuses the normally distinct concepts of particular and general, actual and abstract. The ploughman is a single and specific figure in the landscape, but at the same time he carries significance beyond his singularity, an image of rustic life and human toil, a living descendant of those lying in the graveyard whose lives as symbolic of the human condition in general Gray is to reflect upon in the rest of the poem.

So these opening lines can be read as both the description of a scene and also (as in the case of Coleridge's *Ancient Mariner* discussed earlier) as a setting which keys us in to the theme of the poem as a whole. What is thematically appropriate here is not just the association of the slow closing of the day with the end of life, expressed most evidently by lexical means (*curfew, tolls the knell, parting day, leaves the world*), but also the grammatically signalled representation of a timeless projection of associations from a particular moment in time, events which are perceived as immediate images, but also conceived as abstractions. And, in reference to the points made earlier about the prosodic shape of the verse, the events are expressed both as propositions and as patterns in which movement is held in abeyance while still retaining the intrinsic force of movement.

We might also note that these opening lines do not only key us in to the theme of the poem, but to its mood also. I mentioned earlier that in it Gray departs from the particulars of description to reflect on human life in general, and this reflective mood can itself be read into the separateness of the observations in each line, and into the modification in the noun phrases whose two-syllable structure (*parting day, lowing herd, weary way*) also has the effect of slowing down the metrical movement so that it is suited to the expression of reflective thought.

All of these features of language, phonological, lexical, grammatical, prosodic, then, come together to suggest certain representational readings. We would expect that subsequent verses in the poem could be read as having congruent effects, and, of course, that any alteration to the original would, as before, change the representational scope of the lines. With this in mind, I offer for the reader's consideration the second verse of the *Elegy* in the company of the first, and variants of both. As with the *Ancient Mariner*, there is no space here to discuss, or even to cite, the whole poem, but I hope that readers may be inspired (or at least provoked) to enquire into its meaning for themselves.

> The curfew tolls the knell of parting day,
> The lowing herd winds slowly o'er the lea,
> The ploughman homeward plods his weary way,
> And leaves the world to darkness and to me.
>
> Now fades the glimmering landscape on the sight,
> And all the air a solemn stillness holds,
> Save where the beetle wheels his droning flight,
> And drowsy tinklings lull the distant folds ...

Text A

The curfew tolls the knell of parting day,
The herd is winding slowly o'er the lea,
The ploughman is plodding on his weary way,
Leaving the world to darkness and to me.

The landscape now is fading on the sight,
And all the air a solemn stillness holds,
Save for the beetle wheeling in his flight,
And drowsy tinklings lulling distant folds ...

Text B

A curfew tolls the knell of day,
A lowing herd winds o'er the lea,
A ploughman homeward plods his way,
And leaves the darkened world to me.

Now fades the landscape on the sight,
And all the air a stillness holds,
Save where a beetle wheels his flight,
And tinklings lull the sheep in folds ...

Text C

The curfew ends the day,
The herd winds o'er the lea,
The ploughman plods his way,
And leaves the world to me.

The landscape fades on the sight,
The air a stillness holds,
Save for the beetle's flight,
And tinklings in the folds ...

9 Intertextual associations

What I have been trying to demonstrate in these pages is that in the interpretation of poetry, the severance of connection with context requires the reader to seek significance other than referential by close scrutiny of the text. This brings into focus the intrinsic meanings of the language itself and the way they are realigned as elements of patterns composed within the prosodic form of the poem. So I have talked about *contextual* interpretation, which yields referential meaning, and *textual* interpretation which yields representational meaning. In the former, the significance of what is said depends on the extent to which it engages features of a context which are shared or accessible to those concerned in the communication. Contextual interpretation is, in this sense, essentially *convergent*. Textual interpretation, as I have defined it, allows for the projection of a range of different, contextually unconstrained meanings, and so is essentially *divergent*. The basic point is, then, that freed from the constraint of having to make language fit in with any particular context, poets can exploit the language code itself and fashion its elements into patterns of an alternative order. To interpret poetry is to discern the pattern, and infer its possible significance. But there is another feature of representational meaning which needs to be noticed. I have touched on it earlier (in the discussion of the poem by William Carlos Williams, for example) but I want to bring it to centre stage in the present chapter. I have talked about textual and contextual interpretation; I want now to discuss *intertextual* interpretation.

What I (and others) mean by this is simple enough.[9] If one is attuned to the effect, all texts reverberate with the echoes of other texts. All uses of language have a history of previous uses. Whatever I say or write is a continuation of my experience of language, a kind of recurrence. It is not something which is compiled anew each time by direct consultation of the language code, but composed rather from partially assembled combinations which have previously proved serviceable in similar contexts. But in the usual referential use of language, as I pointed out before, it would be inconvenient for previous contextual uses to be invoked, for this would disrupt the process of convergence on the particular context concerned. The echoes would be an interference on the line which one would normally wish to eliminate so as to tune in more clearly.

Communication, then, is normally effective only to the extent that it is selective of meanings which are recognized as contextually relevant: all other meanings are set aside—not only those which are conventionally established as intrinsic to the code (and recorded in grammars and dictionaries) but also those of individual association that have accumulated through a lifetime of contextual use. This is inevitably the case, for in using language for communication in the ordinary way we enter into a kind of cooperative contract whereby we undertake to achieve convergence on a relevant outcome with the minimum of processing effort.

Since with poetry there is no context to be relevant to, readers are provoked (so I have argued) to find relevance in the way language is textually patterned, and this, as I have tried to demonstrate, involves picking apart and reassembling elements of the code. But readers are also free to conjure up all manner of intertextual associations in their quest for significance, for there is no purpose, no pressure, no obligation to make mutual sense which would otherwise hold them in check. You do not have to reply to a poem, or take action on it, or fit its meaning into the established schemes of socially sanctioned reality. Its meaning is, of its nature, non-accountable. There can be no penalties for misunderstanding, for the normal requirements on understanding simply do not exist.

Let us then consider an example of how intertextual effects can be read into the interpretation of poetry. Here is the opening verse of W.B. Yeats's poem *The Wild Swans at Coole*:

> The trees are in their autumn beauty,
> The woodland paths are dry,
> Under the October twilight the water
> Mirrors a still sky;
> Upon the brimming water among the stones
> Are nine-and-fifty swans.

As in the lines from Gray's *Elegy*, this verse does not only describe a scene, but also sets the poem in a particular key of atmosphere and attitude, and this can be attributed to the resonant effect throughout the lines of words like *autumn* and *twilight*. These reverberate with associations carried over cumulatively from other contexts of use, so that they are not understood in a referential way particular to the occasion but are evocative of experience gathered from all other occasions of reference. *Autumn*—achievement, but only as an ending; ripeness as fulfilment which presages its own decline; beauty which only comes with withering; colours in a final flourish before fading; the mists, the days drawing in, the falling leaves, a chill in the air and signs of approaching winter, and so on. *Twilight*—the setting sun, the close of day, lengthening of shadows and the onset of darkness, time slowing down and sounds settling into silence, people going home, the prospect of rest, and so on. Associations of this kind spread out pervasively from these words and provide an appropriate aura for the poem. Or take the word *swan*. It, too, has associative meanings, congruent with those of *autumn* and *twilight*, and quite other than those of, say, *goose* or *duck*. Quite apart from distinctions of denotation, they have differences of customary contextual occurrence and so give rise to different resonances.

Consider, for example, the appearance of the word *swan* in the opening lines of Tennyson's poem *Tithonus*:

> The woods decay, the woods decay and fall,
> The vapours weep their burthen to the ground,
> Man comes and tills the field and lies beneath,
> And after many a summer dies the swan.

As has been pointed out (by Aldous Huxley), the effect of the last line would be changed quite radically, and would be incongruent, and incongruous, if it were to read:

> And after many a summer dies the duck.

The cumulative associations which set up such resonances come not only from the countless times these words have been used in reference, but also from our experience of other literary texts. Anyone who has read Keats's *Ode to Autumn*, for example, will naturally be disposed to read other poems on that subject against the background of that experience. There are times when this more specific intertextual relationship is quite clearly marked in the text itself, and is directly invoked. Thomas Hood's *Autumn*

Ode, for example, resounds very clearly with verbal echoes from Keats. Here are the opening lines:

> I saw old Autumn in the misty morn
> Stand shadowless like Silence, listening
> To silence, for no lonely bird would sing
> Into his hollow ear from woods forlorn.

The question arises as to what extent recognizing the specific intertextual relationships enhances interpretation. This depends on whether such recognition can be read as relevant, that is to say, as congruent with the meaning assigned to other features of the poem. In some cases, writers will indicate that the intertextual connection is intended by incorporating obvious citation in their text. This is not the case with Hood's poem, where the words of Keats are scattered randomly throughout, giving simply the impression of pastiche. If the poem was intended as a variation on a theme of Keats (as in music, an entirely worthy enterprise, though infrequent in verbal art) one would expect the intention to be indicated in some way, and, of course, the reader would be primed to interpret it accordingly. In the case of T.S. Eliot's *The Waste Land*, on the other hand, there is no room for doubt. Not only do we find obvious citations, but the poem is provided with a set of notes to refer the reader to the original sources. Take these lines, for example:

> Sweet Thames, run softly till I end my song,
> Sweet Thames, run softly, for I speak not loud or long.
> But at my back in a cold blast I hear
> The rattle of the bones, and chuckle spread from ear to ear ...

The first line (as Eliot's notes acknowledge) is a direct quotation from Spenser's *Prothalamion*, the second is a variation on it, and the third draws phrases directly from Marvell's *To His Coy Mistress*. It is clear that Eliot's text is a kind of verbal collage, and that its interpretation is meant to be dependent on our invoking the originals and reading a significance into the way extracts from them have been worked into the pattern of the poem as a whole.

In the case of another poem by Eliot, on the other hand, intertextual recognition would appear to have little bearing on interpretation. I refer to *Journey of the Magi*. The opening five lines of this poem were, when first published, placed within inverted commas, as follows:

'A cold coming we had of it,
Just the worst time of the year
For a journey, and such a long journey:
The ways deep and the weather sharp,
The very dead of winter.'

The inverted commas indicate not direct speech (the first-person narrative continues without them) but direct quotation, for the lines are closely derived from a piece of prose from a sermon given by the Bishop of Winchester, Lancelot Andrewes, before King James in 1622. The original runs as follows:

> It was no summer progress. A cold coming they had of it at this time of the year, just the worst time of the year to take a journey, and especially a long journey in. The ways deep, the weather sharp, the days short, the sun furthest off, *in solstitio brumali*, 'the very dead of winter'.

This time there are no notes to direct us to this source, which would seem to suggest that the poet does not himself feel that the significance of his lines depends on intertextual recognition. This is perhaps as well since there cannot be many readers who would be acquainted with the original.

But how far can the significance of a poem depend on intertextual recognition anyway? What if the language in a poem does not resonate for us with verbal echoes, either from multiple contextual uses, or from a specific textual source? Does this mean that the significance of the poem is lost on us, that our interpretation will be invalid? It would seem on the face of it that these intertextual aspects restrict the accessibility of poetry, narrow its appeal, and sustain its status as reserved text which only the privileged can appreciate. But it is just such a concept of poetry which I have said earlier (in Chapter 1) it is the purpose of this book to counteract. If poems resound with echoes that only some people are attuned to hear, then how can their meaning be apprehended by others who are not so attuned?

One answer to this is that since poetic meaning is, of its very representational nature, unbounded, there can be no criteria for what counts as a valid reading. People with different linguistic and literary experience will read different meanings *into* a text. If we do not identify an expression as a literary citation or allusion, then we cannot, obviously, interpret it as such. But then we will simply interpret it in another way. It is, of course, true that the wider the range of our experience of contextual uses of language and of literary texts is, the more scope there will be for reverberant associations, but this does not validate one response and invalidate another. There can be no definitive interpretation. The point of poetry (indeed the point of all art) is, as I have argued earlier, that it denies authority. It is sadly ironical, therefore, that the teaching of poetry so often imposes authority in the name of critical expertise. This is not to say that literary criticism has nothing to offer, but its contribution has to do, I believe, not with the provision of interpretations but with the process of interpreting. Its value, like the value of the kind of stylistic analysis I have been demonstrating in this book, depends on the extent to which it helps people to make poems their own by individual response.

There is one further point about intertextual associations, and it is one which will take the discussion (in the next chapter) into the matter of aesthetic value. It is this: the absence of contextual constraint allows the reader to let the mind loose to range over possible meanings in free association, but the very patterning of language in verse (even so-called free verse) carries the implication of order. The poem, therefore, poses a kind of challenge: how can all this proliferation of possible meanings be made coherent? For the intertextual association of particular expressions with experience of language *outside* the poem has somehow to be read as consistent with the textual association of these expressions with others *inside* the poem. What poetry does is to suspend the usual contextual constraints so as to suggest textual constraints of its own devising, setting the mind free so that it can more effectively realize meaning within different limits, within a different order of significance. The essential point about poetry is that no matter how unbounded and elusive the meanings are that it releases, these do not randomly disperse but are somehow contained and made coherent within its patterns of language. Like the Indian god Siva, poetry is both destroyer and creator, undermining the conditions necessary for reference in order to create the conditions necessary for representation.

10 Aesthetic effects and relative values

In an earlier chapter of this book, I expressed the view that the modest graveyard inscriptions with which I began should be acknowledged as kin to the grander works of established poets and (in Auden's words) 'share in the total literary glory'. In the preceding chapter I have argued against privileged interpretations, and have taken the position that there are no criteria, except those imposed by fiat, which can assign different values to variable responses. But does this mean that all poems are aesthetically equal, that claims to superior artistic quality are unfounded, that the odes of Keats, say, or the sonnets of Shakespeare, are only accounted great poetry, and other poetic efforts dismissed as lightweight, because those in a position to set standards of excellence have told us so? One might accept that doggerel is kin to works like these, but surely they are *humble* kin, remote country cousins with no rights to any artistic heritage in the poetic tradition.

What is it, then, which constitutes aesthetic quality? How can we make a judgement about the relative artistic value of different poems? I would suggest that the point made in the preceding chapter about the poetic containment of divergent meanings provides us with at least a partial answer. It seems to me that the aesthetic effects of a poem (as with other forms of art) depend on the satisfaction of two conditions. The first is that it disperses meanings and disrupts established ideas, or what T.S. Eliot referred to as 'stock responses'. This (following the reference to Siva in the preceding chapter) we might call the destructive or divergent condition. In respect to this condition, the greater the incongruity of the poem, the more difficult it is to accommodate within accepted structures of reality, and therefore the more variable responses it evokes, the greater its aesthetic potential. But this condition alone would lead us to equate artistic quality with obscurity: the more incomprehensible a poem, the better it is. We need the second condition. This is that the incongruity of the poem and the disruption it causes have to be made congruous, the disorder reassembled into a different order. Its lines have to bring about realignment, so that the divergence of response is made coherent within their limits. This we might refer to as the convergent condition. In respect to this condition, the more patterning that one can discern within a poem, and the more integrated the patterns, the greater its aesthetic potential. But again, it is clear that this condition alone will not do: it will lead us to equate artistic quality with regularity of form.

It is easy to think of poems which, indulgent of idiosyncratic associations or composed for a restricted community of like minds, are maximally divergent in this sense; poems which stimulate all manner of diverse associations, but leave readers with a scatter of diffuse impressions which they cannot relate back to the poem and reassemble into any pattern of significance. When reconvergence is frustrated in this way, one possible solution is to give readers information about the individual or the community in question so that they are better able to realize the conditions of poetic meaning. This, of course, raises the question of how far the interpretation of a poem should depend on the local circumstances of its composition. One could argue (as I would be disposed to argue) that the provision of such information can actually counteract the poetic conditions themselves, in that it has the effect of making a poem in some degree contextually dependent and so making it correspondingly referential. Such consequences are apparent in a good deal of poetry teaching, where poems are used as biographical and historical texts which document the ideas, life, and times of the poet. A preferable approach, one which sustains the artistic integrity of poetic texts, and is consistent with the arguments I have been putting forward in this book, would be to encourage readers to first infer their own uninformed meanings, and only provide further referential information as the occasion required, and as a way of stimulating alternative interpretations.

Just as there are poems in which (for particular readers at least) it is the divergent condition which dominates, so there are others of the opposite convergent tendency. Here we find the appearance of poetry, but little of its significance, artifice without much discernible art. Such poems do not have the effect of releasing the mind in quest of something new, but of enclosing it within what is given. The fashioning of verbal patterns serves only to confirm established ways of thinking. The following is, I think, a good example of a poem which is particularly convergent in this sense:

> The ivory tusk and the feathery breast
> The bird on the wing and the egg in the nest.
> The sap in the tree and the life in the cell
> The wool on the lamb and the pearl in the shell.
> The bee in the hive and the grape on the vine.
> The root in the earth and the gold in the mine.
> The babe in the womb and the seed in the pod.
> The marvels of Nature. The wonders of God.
> (Patience Strong: *Nature's Miracles*)

The tightly knit patterning of metrical regularity, exact rhyme, and lexical and grammatical correspondences expresses a conformity with an orthodox view of the world. The poem is a celebration of the commonplace. There are no surprises. Everything is in its proper and appointed place in the natural order. There is no room for divergence. The wool is (where else?) on the lamb, the bee is, predictably, in the hive, and the grape is just where we would expect it to be: on the vine. The reality which is represented here corresponds exactly to that of ordinary reference. So what, one might ask, is the point of writing a poem?

One answer might be that the point is precisely the affirmation of a belief in the essential rightness and stability of the grand design of the Divinity: God's in his heaven, all's right with the world. But this very phrase is a quotation from a poem by Browning, a song from *Pippa Passes*, where similar sentiments are expressed in very different terms:

> The year's at the spring,
> And day's at the morn;
> Morning's at seven;
> The hillside's dew-pearled;
> The lark's on the wing;
> The snail's on the thorn:
> God's in his heaven—
> All's right with the world!

Although, as with the Wordsworth poem we considered earlier, one might not wish to make any great artistic claims for this little piece, it does offer a degree of divergence, and provokes an enquiry into significance. Again, as with the Wordsworth poem, its simplicity is deceptive. One might note, for example, the way periods of time in the first three lines are drawn to a single point in the present (*year, spring, morning, seven*), so that all time is represented as enclosed within one moment. One might read significance into the association, marked by structural and metrical equivalence, of the lark and the snail, one in the sky, the other on the ground, and see it as suggestive of the harmony between heaven and earth which the song celebrates, and which is proclaimed in the last lines: 'God's in his heaven, all's right with the world.' Pippa's world, with the lark on the wing, and the hillside dew-pearled, is very different from that of Patience Strong, where the bird is on the wing, and the pearl is in the shell. The Browning poem does not confirm the rightness of the world, but creates it.

To indicate the artistic limitations of a poem like that by Patience Strong is not to deny it all value. It is easy to sneer, but one has to remember that countless readers have found pleasure and point in these verses, reassured by the verbal design which expresses an affirmation of faith in the established order. In similar fashion, the gravestone inscriptions we began with can provide solace by the very fact that they give form, and therefore meaning, to the bewildering confusion of bereavement. After all, if people are in an agony of doubt or distress the last thing they want is more disruption in their lives. They need the comfort of convergence. Poems which provide this have their place. It has to be recognized that there are circumstantial limits to the appreciation of art: there is a dependence on detachment, and demands on concentration which cannot be sustained for long. As W.H. Auden puts it:

> Much as he would like to
> Concentrate completely
> On the precious Object,
> Love has not the power;
> Goethe put it neatly:
> No one cares to watch the
> Loveliest sunset after
> Quarter of an hour.
> *(Heavy Date)*

There is a further point to be made. This has to do with the circumstances not of a poem's reading but of its writing. Earlier, when discussing poems which erred in the divergent direction, I suggested that their obscurity could be counteracted by providing additional circumstantial information, but argued that this could have the effect of altering the representational nature of the text. Much the same point can be made of poems which err in the convergent direction. A poem of crude or rudimentary cut, of little apparent divergent effect, can be invested with significance in the light of what we know of its author and the circumstances of its composition. For example, in reading through a book called *New Poetry 1962*, a prestigious annual anthology of contemporary verse, I came across the following poem by somebody called Raymond Richardson:

Railwaymen

Admitting that we were a different lot,
One man put his finger on the spot:
When other people are on holiday
We are working, taking them away,
Which is a very deadening circumstance:
They dub us dull. Comes our turn to dance,
We plunge headfirst into a world nose-down
On the grindstone, no one playing clown
But ourselves: we have a drink, a bet,
I never saw a railwayman yet,
After many years of this dire quenching,
Who didn't have a face like an engine.

This struck me as a pedestrian piece of verse: no resonances here, nothing to engage the imagination, dull indeed. Then I turned to the notes on contributors at the back of the book, and read this:

RAYMOND RICHARDSON was born in 1914, of a family of steelworkers. He was self-educated, having failed to pass the Secondary School examination. He had a variety of jobs; in addition to fifteen years as a railwayman, he worked as a printer's devil, gardener, dairyman, hotel porter, and brickyard labourer. Although he wrote poetry all his life, he was very secretive about his work and always destroyed his poems after they had been rejected. The only poems of his to be published previously were *Bad Taste* and *Fear Of Fog* in the first P.E.N. anthology in this series, *New Poems—1952.* Raymond Richardson died last spring before learning that a third poem of his had at last been accepted for publication in *New Poems—1962.*

This information obviously gives the poem a poignancy that it would not otherwise have, and might dispose us to seek significance in a second reading. But the poignancy is essentially in the referential facts about the poet. It does not follow that we can trace any representational effects in the poem. For representation in poetry, and in all art, as I have argued throughout these pages, has its own conditions to meet, its own reality to create.

11 So the meaning escapes ...

The reality which is represented in poems, fashioned in patterns of language detached from context and reassembled into a different order, is a reconciliation of contraries. It is both particular and general, private and public, actual and abstract, divergent and convergent, fleeting and yet held in perpetual poise. It must of its nature elude any account in referential terms. It is a reality which cannot be explained but only expressed and experienced through the expression. It seems appropriate, therefore, to conclude the discussion of this part of the book with what I read as a representational argument about the very nature of this elusive reality, a kind of meta-poem, a poem about poetry and the meaning of art. It is a poem by Wallace Stevens called *Metaphors of a Magnifico*.

> Twenty men crossing a bridge,
> Into a village,
> Are twenty men crossing twenty bridges,
> Into twenty villages,
> Or one man
> Crossing a single bridge into a village.
>
> This is old song
> That will not declare itself ...
>
> Twenty men crossing a bridge,
> Into a village,
> Are
> Twenty men crossing a bridge
> Into a village.
>
> That will not declare itself
> Yet is certain as meaning ...

The boots of the men clump
On the boards of the bridge.
The first white wall of the village
Rises through fruit-trees.
Of what was it I was thinking?
So the meaning escapes.

The first white wall of the village ...
The fruit-trees ...

Here I find the characteristics of poetic writing that I have been trying prosaically to describe represented with particular aptness. An event is called to mind, and as it is, conceptions of it shift and change in perplexing ways. The third-person observer sees twenty men, one bridge, one village. But each man is an individual and not just one of a number, and so there are also, from this point of view, twenty bridges and twenty villages, an accumulation of individual perceptions. And at the same time, of course, if we take each perception separately, for each man there is just one bridge and one village. The plural and singular propositions are equivalent. We can read these lines as an attempt to rationalize by logical statement the kind of reconciliation between the particular and the general which is represented in the lines from Gray which were discussed earlier. But reasoning leaves the disparity of perspectives unresolved. The meaning of the event remains elusive (it will not declare itself) and the only certainty is the tautology. In the attempt to diverge in quest for significance, we are drawn back to converge on the commonplace, and we cannot capture the coincidence of singular and plural, particular and general realities. So we move from abstract generalities in the first three sections of the poem to actual particulars in the fifth. The definite article now makes a first appearance, and the simple present tense shifts the event into a different temporal key: previously occurring through a period of time (*crossing*), it now occurs at a point in time (*clump*). The event becomes immediate, actual; details come into focus (*the boots of the men, the boards of the bridge*) and are discerned as specific (*The first white wall*) almost as if filmed in close-up. The trees become fruit-trees.

But the actuality is deceptive, for it, too, is unstable, not certain as meaning. For like the preceding abstraction, it is expressed in potentially conflicting singular and plural terms: plural/plural (*boots/men*), plural/singular (*boards/bridge*), singular/singular (*wall/village*) and singular/plural (*wall/trees*). And although the trees become fruit-trees, the noun phrase itself reverts to the indefinite, and signals a transition back to abstraction and the elusiveness of meaning in the last two lines of this section of the poem. The particulars deflect thinking and the meaning escapes because perceptions can only have meaning in a rational sense if they are related to some conceptual generality, abstracted from the immediacy of experience. But such conceptual generality reduces the experience and leads back to the paradox we started with. We are left only with fragments of actual perception in the last two lines: two definite noun phrases that indefinitely lead nowhere . . .

The first white wall of the village . . .
The fruit-trees . . .

So far I have focused on the possible significance of the grammatical features of the text, but we need also to take note of the meanings which are released by the lexis, and the associative resonances of the words. What does the title mean? It indicates that what is described is to be read as metaphorical, and I have suggested one such metaphorical reading. But why are these metaphors of a *magnifico*? A magnifico is a Venetian nobleman. So what? Is it that the poem expresses a privileged view of reality, vouchsafed only to the artist, aloof from involvement in practical life? Or is the implication that those who seek to impose their own meaning on reality by the exercise of power end up only with tautology or contradiction, resolvable only by an alternative order of art? This second interpretation would seem to be consistent with the event that is described, for the image of twenty men crossing the bridge suggests a squad marching in unison, disciplined into conformity. Who are they, these men? The soldiers of an invading army? Why else would they be crossing the bridge, their boots sounding menacingly on the boards as they approach the village, neat and prosperous with its white walls and its fruit-trees, its own ordered existence about to be violated?

The opposition of different realities that I have read into the grammatical features of the poem can, then, be read too in the images conjured up by the lexis. And so the range of possible significance is extended, the ideas which come from divergent association reconverge on the poem. But the meaning still escapes, of course, because it is elusive of its very nature. The poem cannot declare itself. At the end of it, we are left with incomplete images and intimations of meaning whose very elusiveness is held stable, momentarily and for always, in the unique expression of the poem itself.

12 In summary

What I have been seeking to do through the preceding pages is to characterize the nature of poetry and to indicate an approach to its understanding which allows access to its significance without compromising its integrity as verbal art. *What* poems mean cannot be explained, but *how* they mean can be, and such explanation, I would argue, provides the general conditions for individual interpretation. There is a common view that to subject a poem to analysis, and to be explicit about its language, is to diminish its effect and deny its mystery. My view is that, on the contrary, it increases the effect by stimulating an engagement with the poem and extending the range of possible response. The very attempt to be explicit, to provide textual warrant for a particular reading, makes one all the more aware of the dimensions of meaning which must always remain mysterious. Nothing makes us more perceptive and appreciative of the unaccountable than the attempt to account for it. The mystery of poetry, and of art in general, is enhanced by being demystified.

To reduce what I have been saying to terms of stark summary: poetry is a representation of socially unsanctioned reality through the exploitation of unrealized possibilities in language. Two questions arise. Firstly, why should such representation warrant our attention? Most people seem to get by well enough without reading poetry and when it does figure at all in their lives it does so marginally in the modest verses of gravestones and greetings cards, the rudimentary recognition of the rites of passage of birth, marriage, and death. If poetry is so peripheral, how can we justify its inclusion in the school curriculum? It would appear that the effect of including it in the past has been more or less to guarantee that people will exclude it from their lives as soon as they leave school. What, then, is the point of poetry? This question leads us to a consideration of its role in education. The second question is a pedagogic one. If we can define the educational role of poetry in reference to its nature as representation, what approach to teaching it will lead students to a realization of its significance? It is the purpose of the second part of this book to enquire into these questions.

PART TWO

The teaching of poetry

1   The point of poetry

What is the point of poetry? What reasons can there be for retaining it as something to be taught in schools? It still clings on in the curriculum with the tenacity of tradition, protected by some vague notion that, like religious education, it is somehow morally uplifting and good for the soul. True, its prominence has diminished of late, and it is sometimes smuggled in by the back door in disguise, but it is still there. And in universities, of course, (in many countries at least) it remains a very weighty presence, sustained, it would seem, not so much by any cogent rationale as by the inertia of convention. So what rationale might there be for persisting with poetry as a subject for study in schools and universities? What rationale might there be for including literature at all in the curriculum, if it comes to that?

It is hard to make out a convincing case for inclusion if you apply the measures of accountancy which characterize a good deal of educational policy at present. Whatever the value of poetry might be, it cannot be equated with cost-effectiveness. It cannot instruct you in anything which you can turn to material advantage: it does not train you to do anything useful, it provides you with no knowledge or skills which you can use to further your own employment prospects or contribute to the national economy. Unlike science it is not serviceable. In this respect poetry is a poor investment: it has no practical pay-off. It is something which, no doubt, it would be nice to have in the best of all possible worlds but which is an indulgence in the competitive world of business and commerce in which we actually live. At a pinch one might argue that literary prose might conceivably be used to develop some of the reading and writing skills which can be directed to practical purposes. But poetry? We can dispense with that and turn our minds to more serious matters.

It must be conceded, I think, that poetry has no place in manpower planning, in the provision of the operative skills needed to sustain the institutional fabric of the state. Oscar Wilde asserted (in the preface to *The Picture of Dorian Gray*) that 'all art is quite useless'. He was not far wrong. But this does not mean that art has no value: only that its value cannot be calculated in terms of its utility. I would argue indeed that, in a sense, its value lies in its very uselessness, and that this is why it is so crucial in education. But in what sense?

Let me recapitulate points made in the first part of this book. We manage our affairs by use of language. We use it to construct a social reality to suit our needs. The reality is only a convenience and we are constantly realigning its categories to accommodate changing circumstances, to make it more serviceable for our security and control. The language sustains an illusion of stability. It classifies things for us, it allows us to tag and docket individual and particular experiences as socially manageable generalities. What is individual and particular is necessarily suppressed in the process, of course, but that is the price to be paid for social security.

We use language, then, to sustain social order. We use it to subscribe to the communal conventions which define the communities in which we live. We could not communicate otherwise. Of course we can question these conventions, and break free of their constraining influence in the name of new enlightenment. But then we devise other conventions to take their place. There is no way of escaping the reduction to generality, the common factors of individual experience, for otherwise social life would not work at all. And so we join a kind of conspiracy of assumption that the only valid reality is that which is communal, the only truth objective truth, the only experiences which count are those which can be expressed in conventional terms, and all the rest are so much subjective chaff. We know in our heart of hearts, of course, that this is nonsense. We know that there are vast expanses of reality within the awareness of the individual which are beyond the scope of conventional statement. This is what Keats called 'the holiness of the heart's affections and the truth of the imagination'; what Wordsworth described as:

> the soul
> Remembering how she felt but what she felt
> Remembering not.
> *(The Prelude)*

Or, as Pascal put it:

> Le coeur a ses raisons que la raison ne connait point.
> (The heart has its reasons which reason knows nothing of.)
> *(Pensées)*

We talk of the heart and the soul as the closest approximations we can get to referring to such experience, and even to use such words is to risk ridicule. But every individual will attest to its existence. Inchoate and inarticulate as it is, it cannot declare itself, it cannot be referred to. But it can be represented. And that is the point of poetry.

2 Educational relevance; recreation and language awareness

But what is the point of poetry *in education?* Even if one concedes that it represents divergent individual experience in the way I have suggested, it is, surely, of peripheral importance to the practical business of life; a diversion, indeed, a distraction from more urgent and pressing concerns comparable, perhaps, to crossword puzzles or computer games. If this is so, it seems unreasonable to expect that it should figure in the curriculum, except perhaps at a pinch and marginally, more like physical training than physics: a token presence. For the curriculum should surely be designed to service social need, and to prepare children to be maximally effective in institutional life, to satisfy their own aspirations and to meet the requirements of their community. This purpose may indeed involve paying heed to individual development, but as a means to an end, not as an end in itself, something that can be turned to ultimate material advantage, an investment which has an institutional return. One of the first lessons a child learns at school is that there is a great diversity of individual knowledge and experience which does not count as valid in the classroom, and which is indeed suppressed as disruption. But, as I have sought to show, it is just such diversity and disruption that poetic representation is concerned with. All in all, then, it seems only sensible to reduce the educational status of poetry and to include it, if at all, only by tucking it away, as a token relic of cultural tradition, into some relatively insignificant corner of the curriculum.

Not surprisingly, I would take a different view. The diversity of individual experience can never be marshalled into social order, and it will always remain as a potentially subversive force. Attempts to suppress it are likely only to cause it to increase. What seems to be sensible, then, is not to deny it, but to come to terms with it, and turn it to educational advantage. And this, I would argue, is where poetry comes in. It has the potentiality, the *poeten-tiality*, so to speak, to promote diversity which can work to the advantage of both the individual and the social self.[10]

The argument is based on a consideration of two oppositions: work and leisure on the one hand, freedom and constraint on the other. This has rather a grand philosophical ring to it, and sounds pretentious, but the argument is simple enough.

Take the first pair. We generally define leisure negatively as the absence of work, a deserved indulgence in relaxation after effort, ease after toil, pleasure as opposed to profit. Leisure is not something to be taken seriously, for then it becomes indistinguishable from the work which it is meant to be distraction from.

But it is possible, of course, to reverse this view and define work negatively as the absence of leisure. This is not as perverse as it might seem. We have the term 'distraction' as a name for leisure negatively defined, but we also have a term for the positive definition of the notion: 'recreation'. Leisure is the process whereby we re-create ourselves. People talk about recharging their batteries. As is so often the case, the cliché is a popular expression of profound truth. They do indeed recharge their individuality with the force which is expended in the business of social life. Without such recharging or recreation of self, they would shrivel up. If leisure in this recreative sense is denied, individuality will either submit to the spiritual starvation and indeed shrivel; or, driven by the instinct of survival, it will assert itself, and seek creative satisfaction elsewhere. In both cases, the denial has serious social consequences. In the first case, there is inertia in the maintenance of institutional life, since the individual force which is channelled to drive it is debilitated. On the other hand, institutional life is subverted by the individual's quest for creative self-satisfaction which cannot be contained within the established social order.

If we define leisure negatively as distraction, then it is easy enough to dismiss it as peripheral to the concerns of education. But if we define it positively as recreation, it becomes central to such concerns, even if we accept that these are confined essentially to the satisfaction of social rather than individual needs. Of course, education has to prepare people for profitable work. That is necessary. But it is not sufficient. It needs to prepare them also for a recreative use of leisure, not only because otherwise it fails to provide for the exercise of individuality in its own right, indeed as a human right, but also because it otherwise fails to effectively service the requirements of society.

One does not have to look far to find evidence of such failure in the past. But it is, of course, only failure from one point of view. From another, it can be counted as success. For it may be a matter of government policy to make leisure a matter of distraction, and so peripheral to education in general, so as to sustain institutions as the fiefdoms of a minority provided with the necessary individual satisfaction by selective education in the private and privileged sector. If the mass of people can be persuaded that leisure can be equated with distraction, this obviously distracts them also from a quest for recreation, which might be troublesome, and encourages them into supine contentment. One way of reducing individuals, and making them manageable, is to overtly deny them the exercise of individuality: another is to covertly provide them with distraction which gives them little scope for recreative enterprise. These are different modes of suppression favoured by different political systems. But this is a matter which takes me beyond my present brief. The point I want to make here is that leisure as distraction is easy, and often politically expedient, to provide. It is a matter of keeping people in their place by keeping them beguiled by entertainment, by taking their mind *off* things. Leisure conceived of as recreation, on the other hand, involves people putting their mind *to* things, exploring the particularities of individual awareness of the world, giving significant shape to divergent private experience, exercising the prerogative of self without being called to social account.

And this is where poetry comes in, for, as I have argued, it is just such recreation that it represents. I do not want to suggest that it therefore has a monopoly in this regard, and that people ought to spend all their spare time buried in books of poetry. All I want to do is to argue a case for the inclusion of poetry in the curriculum. But this is not meant to imply the exclusion of other things. Clearly, what I have claimed for poetry can apply to literature more generally, and there are other kinds of curricular content and design which can no doubt meet the essential educational requirement of providing for leisure as recreation. But it is my purpose here to argue the particular case for poetry.

And the case is not yet complete. I have talked about the

opposition of work and leisure. There is the second opposition to consider: that between freedom and constraint. In one respect the opposing pairs are similar. The first concept is favoured as having greater value than the second, and this, we might suggest, is indicated by the usual order of appearance of the terms: *work and leisure*, not *leisure and work*; *freedom and constraint* not *constraint and freedom*. So to support the cause of work and freedom is to conform to conventional values; and to speak in favour of leisure and constraint would seem idiosyncratic and perverse. And indeed, it is perverse, for it is surely contradictory to associate leisure with constraint. Leisure is, after all, *free* time. But then it should be equally contradictory and perverse to associate work and freedom, for work generally involves submission to institutional constraints of one kind or another. How, then, are we to reconcile these contradictions?

As before, we need, I think, to give more positive status to the stigmatized concept. Just as before I sought to show that leisure is not simply the absence of work, so now I want to argue that constraint is not simply the absence of freedom. In both cases I believe that we need to recognize that there is a crucial interdependency between the concepts, and this interdependency is a fundamental educational matter which needs somehow to be incorporated into the curriculum. And, of course, I shall argue that one way of doing this is by the inclusion of poetry.

We can begin with the obvious observation that freedom is not absolute but is bound to be relative and is indeed bound by limits: it can only be recognized in reference to its boundaries. We can, and do, argue endlessly about where, and by whom such boundaries should be set, but boundaries there must always be. If this is acknowledged, then, as before with the notion of leisure, we can define constraint in two ways. The negative definition makes constraint a *confinement* which inhibits freedom; the positive definition makes it a *condition* which must be met for freedom to have any meaning at all.

Now, society is in the business of setting boundaries, constraints of rule and convention. Obviously, it could not operate otherwise; and in so doing it provides the necessary conditions for the stability which individuals need to feel secure. Some of these constraints are formally enshrined in legislation: others are matters of conventional custom in behaviour and belief which constitute the culture of a community. There are penalties for non-conformity in each case, and part of the purpose of education is to point this out.

There are two corollaries, two other aspects of such constraints that need to be pointed out as well. One of them is that since they are indeed necessary as conditions for any kind of social stability, any attempt to dispense with them carries with it a commitment to replace them with others. You assert your freedom only to subject it to different delimitations. The second, and related, aspect is that these constraints are of their nature arbitrary conveniences which carry no stamp of absolute legitimacy. So they cannot account for the particulars of human experience: they are simply a set of expedient generalizations which may suit a particular community, but which, equally, may not suit another.

So we might say that social constraints have conditional value in two senses: firstly, in general, they are necessary conditions for the existence of any social life, and secondly, in particular, they are valid only on condition that they are relevant to the community concerned. They are, in short, convenient fictions. Now if we accept this, it follows, it seems to me, that all social constraints should be open to continual question, subjected to critical scrutiny to see whether they are indeed relevant, whether they do indeed function positively as necessary conditions rather than negatively as confinement, maintained by tradition or imposed by the exercise of power. At the same time, we have to recognize that however vigorously we question and challenge, we have eventually to come to terms with the need to restore order by proposing alternative constraints. Indeed, the very questioning and challenging presupposes the acceptance of some set of conventions about what language means and what counts as acceptable modes of argument. Freedom of speech without such constraint would be unintelligible.

Now it seems to me that a crucial part of the purpose of education must be to develop an awareness of the necessary but expedient nature of social constraint, and so to encourage the exercise of conditional freedom in critical enquiry. To be sure, one can simply impose constraint as confinement without bothering to make people aware of its nature, counting on them to defer to authority without question. And in some societies, of course, that is precisely what is done, and indoctrination masquerades as education. I am making what for them would be a quite unwarranted assumption that people should be aware of the nature of the constraints by which they live; recognize, on the one hand, their right to challenge them, and, on the other, their obligation to restore order. For me, this is to say no more than that education should be concerned with preparing people to discharge their role as citizens.

This is all very well, but where, it might be asked, does all this high-sounding argument take us? Even if one concedes that education should prepare for citizenship, as I have suggested, it cannot be claimed, surely, that poetry can contribute to that end. Yes it can. That is precisely the claim I want to make.

I have talked about the individual's right to feel free to challenge the conditions which define that freedom, in other words to diverge; and of the subsequent need to reinstate, or realign or replace them with others to restore order, in other words to converge. I hope that the reader might at this point hear an intertextual echo. For in the first part of this book I used just these terms, divergence and convergence, to describe the essential conditions of poetic representation. I suggested there that poetry, like the god Siva (or like Shelley's *West Wind*, to invoke another text), is both destroyer and preserver, undermining conventional and socially sanctioned reality but preserving the principle of order by recasting reality in a new image held within the patterning of verse. What I want to suggest here is that poetry, representing as it does the reconciliation of the principles of freedom and constraint, can serve to develop a more general awareness of these principles and their relationship in individual and social life.

For you cannot understand poetry, as I have characterized it, without recognizing the arbitrary and expedient character of conventional encodings of reality, the relative inadequacy of all social systems of belief. It is always in some sense a denial of authority and a celebration of divergence. It attracts attention to particular uses of language and allows for diversity of response. As such it encourages the kind of scepticism, recognition of relative validity, and critical scrutiny of established modes of thought and expression which, I have argued, it should be the purpose of education to develop. But equally, you cannot read poetry (again, as I have characterized it) without acknowledging the need for convergence. Quite apart from the fact that the aesthetic response itself depends on the recognition of order of some kind, a convergence without conformity, a reassembly of disparities, the very identification of those disparities in the first place obviously depends on referring them to what is established as normal. The individual freedom of those poet is inevitably constrained by social conventions; they are the necessary conditions for composition since without them the poet could not create special effects by contravening them. And the reader's awareness of the contravention, of course, serves to sharpen awareness of the convention, together with a recognition of the conditional validity of both.

My argument, then, in summary, is this. If education is to be serious about promoting the reciprocal interests of the individual and society, then it has to take into account two relationships. One is between work and leisure, with the latter concept not defined negatively as distraction and marginalized, but defined positively as recreation and seen as a matter of essential regeneration and therefore of central importance for both the individual and society. The second relationship is between freedom and constraint, with the latter concept defined, again positively, as a set of conditions which are necessary, since without them society fragments into anarchy, and the concept of freedom is itself meaningless, but which are at the same time arbitrary and expedient. I argued that getting these relationships right (setting the parameters appropriately, so to speak) is fundamental to the wellbeing of both society and the individual and that developing an awareness of what is involved should therefore be central to the educational enterprise. The importance of poetry as part of the curriculum lies in the potential it has for developing this awareness, since, by virtue of its nature as representation (as this is described in the first part of this book), it is recreative and draws attention to the necessary but expedient conditions on all conventional modes of thought and expression.

Three further points and I am done with this discussion on the educational value of poetry. The first is one I have referred to in passing earlier. It is that I am not claiming that poetry has the exclusive capability of developing the kind of awareness that I have been referring to. I believe that the particular features that poetry has as a use of language make it especially well suited to the purpose, but others might wish to press the claims of their own subject. All I can say is, I only wish they would. There is little sign of interest (in Britain at any rate) in basic questions about educational criteria for curriculum design. People talk a good deal about what should or should not be included in the National Curriculum for subjects like History, English, Modern Languages, and so on, but the debate is almost totally devoid of any consideration of basic educational purpose in respect of the kind of issues I have been raising, and it reduces for the most part to a confrontation of competing prejudices. Indeed, attempts to raise such issues are generally dismissed as an indulgence in vague philosophizing, and the philosophy of education, in fact philosophy of any kind, is generally regarded as irrelevant obfuscation. But these matters are not the business of this book.

I turn to a matter which is: the second of the points I referred to earlier. So far in this part of the book I have been talking about *education*, making out a case for the inclusion of poetry in the curriculum. But, of course, poetry will not have the effects I claim it has the capability of producing simply by being included. Its potential for bringing *about* the kind of awareness I have referred to will only be realized if there is a *pedagogy* which will bring *out* its educational value, an approach to teaching it which is appropriate for the purpose. This takes us on to the next chapter and to a major item on our agenda.

Meanwhile, there is a third point to mention in this chapter. In the first part of this book I talked about the nature of poetry and illustrated my argument exclusively by citing examples of poetry in English. In this part I have talked about the place of poetry in the curriculum. A number of questions arise. First: am I talking about the nature of poetry in English or about poetry in general? The answer here is: poetry in general, or at least lyric poetry in general. I am assuming that the distinctive features that I have tried to identify apply to poetry in whatever language, although there will obviously be differences within the genre (some of which we will be looking at later on). Second: am I talking about the educational role of poetry in general or about the role of poetry in English? The answer here is: the educational role of poetry in general. I am assuming that the issues I raised about the individual and society and the pairs of opposing concepts have general relevance, although, of course, different circumstances will require different policies as to how these issues are to be resolved. Third: am I talking about poetry in a first or a second language? The answer here is that the educational effect that I am claiming would be primarily achieved through first-language poetry, although second-language poetry cannot be discounted, especially not in the case of advanced learners. Second-language poetry can be effective for the development of language awareness and ability, as I shall try to demonstrate. As with the discussion in the first part of this book, I am assuming that although the demonstration of pedagogy that follows will make exclusive use of poems in English, the principles of approach will be applicable to poems in other languages.

3 Pedagogic approaches; against exegesis

Poetry, as I have characterized it in the first part of this book, can, I have just argued, claim a place in the curriculum on the grounds that, in principle, it has the potential for realizing fundamental educational objectives. A potential in principle. That is all very well, but how might the potential be realized in practice? What kind of classroom activity can be proposed which will be an effective means towards this desired end? We turn to the question of appropriate pedagogy.

We can begin by dispensing with ways of teaching poetry which, whatever merits they might otherwise have, are counter to what I have been proposing, and so cannot serve our purpose. This would seem to eliminate at once any approach which equates the meaning of a poem with its paraphrase or any which disregards individual response to the text in favour of definitive explanations sanctioned by critical authority. The first reduces representation to reference by making the poetic text equivalent to a description of its content, and so confirms the values of established convention. The second makes the poetic text equivalent to an explanation of its meaning and so prevents diversity of interpretation: the reader is instructed in the expert commentaries of others, rather as Alice is instructed about the meaning of the poem *Jabberwocky* by Humpty Dumpty, who makes the somewhat excessive literary critical claim that he can 'explain all the poems that ever were invented—and a good many that haven't been invented just yet' (Lewis Carroll: *Through the Looking-Glass*).

In both of these cases, the essential nature of poetry is denied, and consequently there are no educational effects of individual recreation or the recognition of the conditional character of established modes of thought.

Each of these lines of approach can be contrasted with others of opposite tendency. Thus, instead of supposing that the meaning of a poem can be captured by paraphrase, one can suppose that it is uniquely but elusively projected from the poem. This, of course, is the view expressed in this book. But it is quite commonly inferred, as a corollary, that this meaning is so mysterious and remote that it can only be revealed like religious experience by some inexplicable process of imaginative osmosis. You should not tamper with the text, for to do so is to violate its sanctity. Analysis is anathema, an act of desecration. In Wordsworth's words (and being a poet he should be an authority on the subject):

> Our meddling intellect
> Mis-shapes the beauteous forms of things;
> We murder to dissect.
> *(The Tables Turned)*

The view expressed in this book is, of course, quite different. And I do not accept, anyway, that poets have any special authority to pronounce on the nature of poetry, any more than linguistic ability gives you any special authority to talk about linguistics. I would accept that poetic meaning is indeed mysterious, but this for me would be a reason for *not* protecting it from analysis. For, as I have argued earlier, analysis can have the effect of enhancing the mystery by making clear the limits of what is explicable. Analysis is not the same as dissection: for it always involves a reconstitution of some kind, dismantling something in order to reassemble it in a different form. In this sense, analysis is always creative, and it is for this reason that its application to poetry can serve a recreative purpose in education. Everything depends, of course, on how it is done and who does it. But at all events, if a poem is treated like sanctified script, there is no way in which students can actually engage with it as individuals and make it their own as an experience of conditional reality: they can only be affected by it as the expression of some transcendental truth. Furthermore, as in the case of other sanctified things, poems are protected by the appointment of custodians who are thought to have privileged access to their significance. There is thus an easy transition to the second approach to poetry that I have mentioned: the deference to the high priests or Humpty Dumpties of critical exegesis. You cannot understand poetry directly, but only through the mediation of those who have been initiated into its mysteries. This third way of thinking of poetry, in many respects in opposition to the first, can be seen to be, in other respects, consistent with the second. And none of them looks to be congruent with the ideas about poetry and its educational value that I have been propounding.

What of the fourth that I referred to earlier? This, as I indicated, is in opposition to the second. Here the denial of critical authority and the recognition of the legitimacy of diverse interpretatations inspires the heady idea that readers can make poems mean whatever they like without giving any warrant for their individual response by reference to features of the text. Anything goes. This too calls Humpty Dumpty to mind. For he not only claims expertise, but he does so by the assertion of arbitrary subjectivity:

> 'When *I* use a word,' Humpty Dumpty said, in rather a scornful tone, 'it means just what I choose it to mean—neither more nor less.'

But just as (in reference to an earlier point) mystery is meaningless unless it is set against what can be explained, so diversity is meaningless unless it is set against what can be agreed. Every poetic text, however divergent it might be, contains features which have to be recognized as matters of common consent. Poetry is not like pottery: it is not shaped out of some primal substance like clay. It is made out of a particular language, composed from a code, and so however curiously it is fashioned, the language retains traces of its conventional origin. You could not, of course, recognize the curiosity otherwise. As I tried to demonstrate earlier in the book, in poetry two kinds of linguistic patterning coexist, one superimposed on the other, and both held in a poised equilibrium: that which is created within the context of the poem itself and that which is conventional to the code. A word or feature of grammar cannot take on contextual life of its own in the poem in disregard of what it conventionally means. Representation can only be recognized in relation to reference. So it is simply perverse to say that a poem can mean anything. There are aspects of any poem that *can* be reduced to paraphrase. What is of interest is what cannot. So we need to establish consensus in order to be aware of what is beyond its limits. This is fundamental to an understanding of poetry, and fundamental too to its educational potential. For what we are talking about here is precisely this question of constraints as conditions on the exercise of individual freedom. Interpretation is constrained by the text, for otherwise there could be no interpretation at all, just as individuality owes its very significance to the constraints which are socially imposed. A way of thinking about poetry which encourages the idea of absolute freedom (anything goes) misrepresents the nature of representation, and, in consequence, negates its educational value.

There are, then, reasons for rejecting all four of these lines of approach to the extent that they are proposed as separately sufficient ways of developing an understanding of poetry, and of realizing its educational potential. But this does not mean that they cannot be turned to pedagogic advantage. For they suggest classroom activities which can draw attention to the very limitations which I have noted. Thus, we can get students to consider paraphrases of a poem, or to write their own, not as a way of *capturing* its significance, but of making them aware of how *elusive* it is, and of drawing their attention to features of the original text that do not survive reformulation into prose.

Similarly, there is no reason, in principle, for denying students access to literary critical opinion—but as a means of provoking them to provide interpretations of their own. The difficulty is, of course, that this opinion is usually so invested in prestige that it has exactly the reverse effect. Students are not encouraged to question it and there are penalties for denying its authority. Who are they to challenge the pronouncements in print of experts in exegesis? Thus the primary texts for study in so many cases are not those of literature but those of literary criticism, and so the whole point and purpose of poetry are lost. But it does not have to be so. There is a legitimate use for such texts as catalysts of enquiry.

As to the idea that anything goes, it could be an effective tactic to encourage students to indulge in free subjective response and to give their immediate impressions of what a poem is about. But this, I suggest, is only the beginning and not the end of the matter. The impressions need then to be discussed, substantiated, and compared for cogency in reference to textual evidence. As common ground is thus established by consensus, the scope for individual diversity of interpretation becomes clear and meaningful by the very limits which define it. In this way, students make the poem more securely their own. Again, the point is that the constraints serve as conditions for meaning, and one of the ways of bringing this home to students is to begin permissively by setting no constraints whatever.

What about the sanctity of the poetic text? This notion can clearly have no place in the scheme of things that I am proposing, which is based on the contrary notion that only when a text is unsanctified can it have significance for individual readers. But the notion is widespread and it commonly has a powerful deterrent effect on students. One way of counteracting this effect is to encourage students to be disrespectful, to let them suggest impertinent amendments to the text, write ribald parodies and in general recast poems as alternative versions in a more familiar and popular idiom. The prevalence of graffiti in the vicinity of schools suggests that, once given licence, students should have no difficulty with this kind of recreation and would take delight in it. It is one obvious way for them to make a poem their own. And since poetry does not depend on sanctity, but, on the contrary, is generally stifled by it, it will not only survive the desecration but be the better for the experience.

What I suggest we are looking for, then, are activities which will engage students with poetic texts and draw their attention to the possible significance of particular linguistic features as conditions on interpretation. Such activities would be designed to bring out the representational nature of poetic meaning and so to fulfil the recreational purpose of education, as I have defined these concepts. So much for the abstract theory of the thing. We need now to consider how this might work out in actual practice. It is time for examples.

What follows is a series of activities. They are proposed in no fixed order: they can be selected from and combined in whatever ways seem suitable. I should add, too, that they are not meant to be tied to particular poems, but to be illustrative of more general application.

There are two further points about these activities which I should make clear. In the first place, they are not original. Over recent years a number of books have appeared which use activities of this kind for the integration of language and literature teaching.[11] My purpose here is to demonstrate and discuss them as techniques which realize the principles of poetentiality and educational relevance which I have proposed. What I have tried to do is to analyse these practices as applications of theory. In this way I hope that what I have to say lends support to the admirable pedagogic work already done by other people.

The second point is that it is not suggested that these activities should exclude all others. As I indicate in what follows, there are several ways in which students can be primed to read literature, including the exploration of the imaginative manipulation of language in everyday use, as in advertisements, newspaper headlines, and so on.[12] Such activities would, where appropriate, precede those I am proposing here. And equally there are several ways of extending literary appreciation subsequently. But neither preceding nor subsequent activities are on my present agenda. My concern is to demonstrate the crucial but not exclusive pedagogic role of practical stylistics as expounded in Part One. What I propose in this Part can be seen as providing a transitional phase between the preparatory exploration of imaginative language and the more extensive study of literature proper. How these other phases might be managed I leave to others to suggest.

One final preliminary: the poems I have chosen to work on reflect idiosyncratic preferences and I do not expect them to be to everybody's taste or to be regarded as universally suitable. Which poems it is appropriate to introduce in respect to linguistic complexity, cultural content, intrinsic interest, and so on is a matter for local decision. What criteria for selection should inform such decisions is, of course, an important question, and I shall touch on it in passing in what follows, but it is not one which it is my present purpose to explore.

4 Composing poetic text: line assembly

We may begin with activities which encourage students to assemble a poem for themselves from its component parts. The simplest and least demanding of these is to get the students, individually or collectively, to arrange the scrambled and unpunctuated lines of a poem into what seems to be the most satisfactory sequence. The collective way of doing this is to divide students into groups and give a line to each member of each group. Their task is to compose the poem by group consensus. If the groups come up with different versions, these can then be compared and their relative merits argued for by reference to the textual evidence. Some of the evidence will, of course, take the form of grammatical dependencies and lexical links across lines, and in this respect the activity is a language exercise. But the shape of the poem is not entirely determined by such dependencies and other considerations will come into play: considerations which have to do with the interpretation of literary effect, a sense of what the poem is about, quite apart from what is explicitly signalled.

The activity can be made less demanding by providing part of the poem as a frame within which the remaining lines are to be assembled. It can be made more demanding by including distractors, lines which do not belong to the original poem. Thus, for instance, students might be required to compose an eight-line poem out of a set of, say, fourteen lines. Here is an example. The following is a list of randomly ordered lines, eight of which can be arranged to compose a poem by Edward Thomas. The other six are maverick distractors.

Cock-Crow

1 Out of the night two cocks together crow
2 Across the darkened fields the moon shines bright

3 Cleaving the darkness with a silver blow
4 The boys are playing football in the park
5 Out of the wood where lots of flowers grow
6 Each facing each as in a coat of arms
7 Out of the wood of thoughts that grows by night
8 Heralds of splendour one at either hand
9 I hear the joyful singing of a lark
10 The milkers lace their boots up at the farms
11 To be cut down by the sharp axe of light
12 And bright before my eyes twin trumpeters stand
13 The fields are silent in the early dark
14 Sounding dawn's fanfare to the fields and farms

We could stage the task by asking students to compose a six-line poem first and then look for ways of incorporating the remaining two lines.

Let us then consider some of the processes of inference and argument which students might use to assemble poetry from these sentential parts, having first primed them by discussion or demonstration to look for grammatical and lexical clues, and encouraging them to refer to a dictionary as required.

To begin with, some of these lines are grammatically dependent: thus lines 3, 5, 6, 7, 11, and 14 are phrases that need to be linked up with other lines. They could, for example, go grammatically with lines 1, 2, 4, 9, 10, and 13 to yield pairings like:

A: Out of the night two cocks together crow,
    Cleaving the darkness with a silver blow.

B: I hear the joyful singing of a lark,
    Cleaving the darkness with a silver blow.

C: Cleaving the darkness with a silver blow,
    The boys are playing football in the park.

D: The milkers lace their boots up at the farms,
    To be cut down by the sharp axe of light.

E: I hear the joyful singing of a lark,
    To be cut down by the sharp axe of light.

F: Out of the wood of thoughts that grows by night,
    I hear the joyful singing of a lark.

And so on. There are many combinations. Too many: these

particular dependencies, though suggestive of all sorts of intriguing possibilities, still leave us with unfocused meanings and uncertainties as to composition. Some of the combinations we might be tempted to reject at once on the grounds that they make no sense. But with poems you can never tell.

So we need to look at what clues to composition there might be in other dependencies. The conjunction *and* at the beginning of line 12, for example, signals a continuity from some previous line, so it presumably cannot come first in the poem. Again, the pronoun *each* in line 6 has dual and not plural reference, so it links naturally with either *two cocks* in line 1 or *twin trumpeters* in line 12. But it also links with the dual determiner *either* in line 8, which signals that there are also two *heralds of splendour*.

And now one might look for lexical links between these lines. These might be recognized by some students, discovered by others by reference to a dictionary. Thus *herald* is associated with *trumpeter*. It is also associated with *coat of arms*: the *Oxford Advanced Learner's Dictionary*, for example, has the following entry:

heraldry   study of the coats of arms and the history of old families.

There is also a link with line 3, of course, since producing a blow on a trumpet is just what you would expect a trumpeter to do, and trumpets are commonly silver, at least in appearance. And then there is line 14. This fits in too, for the dictionary entry for *fanfare* reads as follows:

fanfare   short ceremonial piece of music, usually played on trumpets.

Taking all these clues together, then, it is possible to piece a poem together out of lines 1, 3, 6, 8, 12, 14, adding a little punctuation to yield the following:

Text A

Out of the night, two cocks together crow,
Cleaving the darkness with a silver blow:
Each facing each as in a coat of arms:
Heralds of splendour, one at either hand.
And bright before my eyes twin trumpeters stand,
Sounding dawn's fanfare to the fields and farms.

This is one sequence. But there are others which are consistent with the linguistic evidence and which other groups or individuals might produce. For example:

Text B

Cleaving the darkness with a silver blow,
Out of the night, two cocks together crow.
And bright before my eyes twin trumpeters stand,
Sounding dawn's fanfare to the fields and farms:
Heralds of splendour, one at either hand,
Each facing each as in a coat of arms.

Text C

Out of the night, two cocks together crow,
Cleaving the darkness with a silver blow:
And bright before my eyes twin trumpeters stand,
Heralds of splendour, one at either hand,
Each facing each as in a coat of arms,
Sounding dawn's fanfare to the fields and farms.

Of course, some students will not home in on evidence in this way at all. They will pursue other linguistic clues, other impressions and associations, and come up with entirely different versions. The following, for example:

Text D

Across the darkened fields the moon shines bright,
Cleaving the darkness with a silver blow.
Out of the wood of thoughts that grows by night,
Out of the wood where lots of flowers grow,
I hear the joyful singing of a lark.
The fields are silent in the early dark.

This sequence conforms to grammatical requirements. And it makes sense. In the first two lines, we have the effective image of the silver light of the moon cutting through the darkness, with the word *blow* understood this time to mean not, as in the other versions, an act of blowing as on a musical instrument, but as a sharp stroke as with a sword or scythe. In the second two lines, the repeated word *grow* closely associates thoughts and flowers, which seems appropriate enough. The singing of the lark is indeed a feature of the early morning, and it can be said to give emphasis to the silence of the surrounding fields. There is, furthermore, an internal pattern of the phrasal repetition (*out of the wood*) and of lexical connections (*darkened, darkness, night, dark*). And the last line provides a neat closure in that it is a variable echo of words of the opening line (*fields, dark*) and serves as a sort of reprise.

These (and other sequences) can then be compared and their relative merits discussed. But now the focus of attention is not on what is linguistically well formed, for all these versions can be said to be equally 'correct' and cohesive as far as grammatical and lexical connections are concerned. The question now has to do with literary effect. Which version seems to be most satisfactory in respect to the internal patterning of language? Which seems to be the most coherent as the representation of experience? Which of them captures most effectively what the poem is about as indicated by its title?

The question can be raised at this point as to whether any of the other lines in the original set might be incorporated into any of these versions, or whether any of them might provide replacements for the lines that have been composed so far. Some individual or groups may indeed have done so in their versions. Both lines 5 and 7, for example, begin with the phrase *out of the wood* and this is, of course, structurally equivalent to the opening phrase of the first line of Texts A and C. It might make a satisfactory pattern of language to add one of them as a beginning to these versions. Line 5 might be preferred on the grounds that it keys into the rhyme scheme, whereas line 7 does not. But its meaning does not seem to fit:

> Out of the wood where lots of flowers grow,
> Out of the night, two cocks together crow . . .

Why should these two cocks be in the wood, rather than in their more customary habitat of the farmyard? And what is the point of the flowers? They make no further appearance in the poem, and there is nothing in what follows that lends them any significance. They do not seem to represent anything. They lead to a dead end. On the other hand, line 7 is discordant in that it does not rhyme. But help is at hand. We can add line 11. This provides us with the required rhyme. It is structurally dependent, and so is grammatically consistent. And it fits in lexically: *cut down* links to *wood*.

Furthermore, this line links up with what follows in Texts A and C: both *cut down* and *axe* relate to *cleaving*; *light* relates to *night*, *darkness*, and *bright*.

And so, with considerations such as these, we might come up with the required eight-line poem along (quite literally) the following lines:

Text E

Out of the wood of thoughts that grows by night
To be cut down by the sharp axe of light,
Out of the night, two cocks together crow,
Cleaving the darkness with a silver blow:
And bright before my eyes twin trumpeters stand,
Heralds of splendour, one at either hand,
Each facing each as in a coat of arms,
Sounding dawn's fanfare to the fields and farms.

Similar attempts can be encouraged to extend other versions by the inclusion of other lines in the original set.

And all this discussion, this assertion and justification of preferences, will sharpen the students' curiosity about the original. How do their versions compare with what Edward Thomas actually wrote? At some appropriate point, when the students have staked a claim to the poem in advance by their own creative and reflective activities, and are therefore primed to be receptive to it, the original can be revealed, slowly (to sustain the suspense), line by line:

Cock-Crow

1 Out of the wood of thoughts that grows by night
2 To be cut down by the sharp axe of light,—
3 Out of the night, two cocks together crow,
4 Cleaving the darkness with a silver blow:
5 And bright before my eyes twin trumpeters stand,
6 Heralds of splendour, one at either hand,
7 Each facing each as in a coat of arms:
8 The milkers lace their boots up at the farms.

Most of this will probably unfold as a pleasing confirmation. The last line, however, is likely to come as a surprise. Indeed, the preceding discussion of different versions can be (as it has been here) deliberately directed so as to spring the surprise, to conjure this last line, so to speak, out of a hat. So far it has been disregarded as a distractor, almost as incongruous as line 4 (*The boys are playing football in the park*). Yet here it is, part of the pattern of the poem, calling for the incongruity to be somehow made consistent with the rest. All the preceding composing and discussing of different versions will, I suggest, have primed students to consider how the poem, now complete and authorized as the original, might be interpreted. What effect, then, does this last line have? What is its significance for the meaning of the poem as a whole? What do you think Edward Thomas is trying to say?

One might expect that, with appropriate encouragement and guidance, the following kinds of responses might emerge. This last line contrasts with the others in several respects. To begin with, what it expresses, its propositional content, has to do with ordinary everyday reality, quite different from the images invoked in the other lines. It is true that the word *farms* can be associated with *cocks* in line 3, and this after all is where you would expect them to be when they start to crow in the early morning. But up to this point this usual referential association has been deflected by others within the context of the poem which takes these birds out of the farmyard, and represents them grandly as trumpeters, emblems of splendour, heraldic beasts, suggestive of symbolic ceremony and expressive of the elemental, transcendental forces of darkness and light. We have seven lines of high-flown ritual; one of humble routine.

The contrast is not only expressed in the propositions, in the paraphraseable content of these lines, in what can be restated in straightforward referential terms. It is also expressed in ways that cannot be paraphrased. That is to say, the contrast is *represented* in the patterns of language in the poem. Thus, the grammar of the first seven lines is elaborately fashioned in a way which befits ceremony. There are only two main clauses, in lines 3 and 5. But even these are cast in unusual form, as the following comparisons make clear:

Out of the night, two cocks together crow.
Two cocks crow together out of the night.

And bright before my eyes twin trumpeters stand.
And twin trumpeters stand bright(?) before my eyes.

All the other lines are assembled around these clauses as attendant phrases, as adverbials in the first half of the poem, in apposition in the second. These are not arranged to accord with necessary syntactic requirement but disposed to suit the internal design of the poem. As we noticed earlier, it is grammatically possible to order these lines in a variety of permutations (which was why we needed to look elsewhere for guidance in the composing process). We can now suggest a possible significance in this. The patterns are created designs suited to ceremony, not simply grammatical structures constrained by syntax. They are fashioned by art, and are therefore artistic. But they are also, of course, from another point of view, fashioned by artifice and are therefore artificial. The last line of the poem brings us down to earth and confronts us, quite unceremoniously, with everyday reality.

And, appropriately enough, the syntax is simple and straightforward. There is a single main clause, complete in itself, enclosed within the metrical line, and consisting of a regular sequence of constituents. All of the words except one are monosyllables. There is no grammatical elaboration whatever, either in the syntax or in the morphology. Nothing could be more pointedly plain and ordinary.

It is, of course, all the more pointed for being unexpected. And this effect also is achieved by grammatical patterning as well as by the abrupt change of propositional content. Consider the preceding two lines. As far as syntax is concerned they are surplus to requirement, a series of appositional phrases added on to the clause of line 5 which is grammatically complete without them. Since there are no expectations generated from the grammar, the reader can only anticipate a continuation of the artistically fashioned patterning of language created within the context of the poem. We are, so to speak, drawn into the design, and lulled into the security of the ceremonial ritual. When this design is so abruptly disrupted by the sudden breaking in of the last line, it comes as a rude awakening. This, we might suggest, is itself representative of what early morning means to most people: cock-crow (or the alarm clock) is the harsh recall to the bleak reality of daily toil. The splendour is dispelled. The imaginative thoughts that grow by night, and influence the first perceptions of the day, are indeed cut down. The ceremony which celebrates the elemental significance of darkness and light cannot be sustained.

And yet it too has its place in the scheme of things. The vision of splendour and ceremony is not invalid. The last line of the poem does not cancel out the preceding seven. It coexists with them and gives them significance. It indeed completes the pattern of the poem with a last rhyming closure, in a way which it would not, of course, if it took the grammatically equivalent form:

The milkers at the farm lace up their boots.

So although the last line is incongruous in content and structure, it is also a congruent part of the poem as a whole. The contrasting perceptions of the cock-crow are brought together within a unitary representation: the dual reality, fleeting and unstable, is held in a kind of precarious permanence within the poise of the poem's artistic design.

Of course students are unlikely to use such terms to express their interpretation of the poem's meaning. But I believe that the kinds of activity I have proposed can stimulate this kind of interpretative process, however it is expressed, and prepare them furthermore (if need be) to understand and evaluate the comments of literary criticism, which do tend to be couched in such terms. The approach to analysis that I am demonstrating here is meant to be transitional, not to replace the more familiar practices of literary criticism (which the later activities in particular clearly draw upon) but to set up conditions for their more effective application.

It should be stressed, too, that when I talk about interpretation I am referring to the process in general and not a particular and definitive exegesis. There must always be room for alternative and individual readings. And when all is said and done, after the original version has been given this careful consideration, some students might still prefer versions that they have themselves composed. The point is not to suppress alternative readings and versions, but to encourage students to support them with reference to the text, and subject them to discussion so that consensus is taken as far as it will go. It is important for them to see that the possibility of variable interpretations does not provide a licence simply to be whimsical and random in their reactions, that if anything goes, nothing meaningful emerges. Otherwise, as I have argued, both the intrinsic nature of poetry, and its educational purpose are denied.

One further point might be emphasized about these activities. I have made it before, but it will perhaps bear repetition. It is that they are intended to be flexible in application, adjustable in focus and difficulty to suit particular teaching/learning circumstances. For example, the starting point of the demonstration in this chapter was a set of lines which contained those of the Edward Thomas poem in their original form. It is easy to see that we can make the task of composition more demanding by reformulating these by altering the order of their sentence constituents. So, for example, we could replace lines 1, 3, and 8 with the following variants:

> Two cocks together crow out of the night
> With a silver blow cleaving the darkness
> One at either hand, heralds of splendour

Composition would then call for structural adjustment so to achieve the required metre and rhyme. Or, to the same end, we could replace lexical items with synonyms, requiring the students to restore those of the original to make the rhyming fit. Thus we could replace lines 3, 8, and 11 with:

> Cleaving the darkness with a silver blast
> To be cut down by the sharp axe of day
> Heralds of splendour, one on either side

Again, there will be teaching/learning situations which will require more attention to language work; others which will call for more concentration on literary appreciation. These activities allow for variations of emphasis. But the essential point is that in all cases, the language and literature are treated as interdependent: an awareness of linguistic potential is not distinct from a sense of literary effect. This is the principle which derives from the previous arguments about the representational meaning of poetry and its educational value, and which therefore informs the design of the pedagogy demonstrated in this chapter, and in those which follow.

5   Completing poetic text: verse blanks

In the previous activity, students were invited to compose a poem out of component parts. The original was then presented at the end of this process. An alternative tactic is to present the original at the outset, but with certain parts of it removed. The task here is not so much composition as completion: the students are required to fill in the blanks with what they judge to be the appropriate words. This is the activity, familiar to language teachers, which goes under the name of cloze procedure. Considered simply as a language exercise, the completion of the text is done by reference to linguistic knowledge. As in the previous activity, however, there are occasions when this knowledge alone will not suffice to fix on a single and definitive solution. It is at such points when questions of poetic appropriateness arise and language analysis shades into literary appreciation. As before, the difficulty of the task can be regulated in a number of ways. One might, for example, vary the amount of what is missing from the original: one might leave out whole lines, or just the occasional word. Alternatively, or in addition, one might provide a set of possibilities for the students to choose from: a selection of words and phrases in English or in the students' own language. Let us consider an example. In this case, only four words have been removed from the original, and there is no check list of possibilities provided. It is a poem by A.E. Housman.

'Loveliest of trees'

Loveliest of trees, the cherry now
Is hung with ...(1)... along the bough,
And stands about the woodland ride
Wearing white for Eastertide.

Now, of my threescore years and ten,
Twenty will not come again,
And take from seventy springs a score,
It only leaves me . . .(2). . . more.

And since to look at things in bloom
Fifty springs are little room,
About the . . .(3). . . I will go
To see the cherry hung with . . .(4). . . .

I will follow the same vicarious process as before and suggest proposals and arguments which, with prompting and guidance, students might reasonably come up with in class. With reference to gap 1, then, what is it that the cherry tree is hung with? Cherries perhaps? Why not? Certainly it is not likely to be hung with any other fruit. But in line 4 we are told that it is wearing white. Cherries are not (usually) white. Furthermore, they are not likely to be in evidence at this time of the year, which, being Eastertide, is in the spring (as is confirmed in the second and third verses). Some students might not, of course, know this, and we come here against the problem not of knowledge of language but knowledge of the world. We will return to this problem a little later, but meanwhile we need to consider other possible fillers for gap 1. What about *flowers*? They can be white. True. But what do we usually call the flowers of a tree? Blossom. The only difficulty about this word is that, like *cherries* and *flowers*, it has two syllables, and as such somewhat disrupts the metrical rhythm of the line, which we would expect to be regular in accordance with the rest of the poem. At this point, we might refer to the dictionary to see if it provides any more suitable alternative. The entry for *blossom* in the *Oxford Advanced Learner's Dictionary* reads as follows:

blossom   flower, esp of a fruit tree or flowering shrub. Cf
BLOOM.

Bloom. This looks to be a likely candidate. The meaning is appropriate. It is monosyllabic and fits into the metre; and it keys in with the word *bough* by the alliteration of the initial consonant. Furthermore, it patterns in with the recurrence of the same word in the third verse. Let us then pencil it in for the moment, allowing always for the possibility that we may have to amend it later. On, then, to gap 2 in the second verse.

The word *score* in this second verse will be unfamiliar to many students, and they may feel the need to refer to a dictionary. Even then, they may need to be told that the phrase *threescore years and ten* is a biblical reference to the normal span of human life. It should be noticed though, that the filling of gap 2 does not depend on knowing the meaning of the word *score* beforehand. It can be inferred from the context, and students might indeed, as a simple language exercise, be encouraged to do just this: threescore and ten (line 1) minus twenty (line 2) is the same as a score taken away from seventy (line 3). Therefore a score means twenty. A little elementary mathematics will give us the answer we need: seventy minus a score (i.e. twenty) equals fifty. So filling in this gap is a straightforward matter of simple arithmetic calculation. And there can only be one solution. There is no problem here. Equally, it might be objected, there is not much poetry here either. The whole verse is devoted to a statement of the obvious: not quite two and two make four, but not far off it. Why should this be so? The fact that filling in the gap is so unproblematic itself poses a problem about its poetic significance. This is a matter we need to return to. Meanwhile, there are the gaps in the last verse to consider.

All kinds of expressions might be proposed for gap 3: *fields*, perhaps, or *woods*, or *countryside, pathways, leafy lanes*. One of my students even came up with the word *business* (I will go about the business of looking at things in bloom). Is there any way of narrowing down the possibilities? To begin with, if we are to suppose that this line is to be consistent with the metrical regularity of the rest of the poem, we need a word of two syllables. This would key in with the prosody, the sound pattern. But we might also note, in reference to propositional meaning and grammatical patterning, that the word *about* makes an appearance also in the first verse in the phrase *about the woodland ride*, which indicates where these cherry trees are. It would seem to make sense, and to make an appropriate pattern of recurrence, to fill the gap with *woodland ride*. Except that it does not fit prosodically. So why not just use *woodland* on its own? Pencil it in.

The most obvious constraint on choice for gap 4 is prosodic: if it is to complete the poem according to the pattern established so far, it has to be monosyllabic and rhyme with *go*. And in reference to recurrent patterns, it might be noticed that the phrase *hung with...* (like the phrase *about the...* previously discussed) occurs earlier in the poem. But *hung with bloom* will not do, since it does not afford us the required rhyme, and it would, anyway, be a simple and redundant repetition of the word that ends the first line of this verse. *Bloom*, however, gives us a clue. What is represented to us as significant about the cherry tree, what makes it the loveliest of trees, is its blossom, its bloom. And this, we are told in the last line of the first verse, is white. So we are looking for something which hangs on the bough, like blossom, and is white, and which, furthermore (in reference to other lines of the poem), we would not be surprised to find in the season of spring. And the word which satisfies these criteria has to be monosyllabic and rhyme with *go*. *Snow* perhaps? It is time to present the original.

> Loveliest of trees, the cherry now
> Is hung with bloom along the bough,
> And stands about the woodland ride,
> Wearing white for Eastertide.
>
> Now, of my threescore years and ten,
> Twenty will not come again,
> And take from seventy springs a score,
> It only leaves me fifty more.
>
> And since to look at things in bloom
> Fifty springs are little room,
> About the woodlands I will go
> To see the cherry hung with snow.

Homing in on appropriate words to fill the gaps requires close attention both to the propositional content and to the patterning of language in the poem. In this way, students practise the usual referential procedures which would be applicable to any text, but also take into account the prosodic features of metre and rhyme which are peculiar to poetry. As before with composition, so here with completion, the task depends on and develops an awareness of both linguistic and literary significance. And, again as before, students are primed by their own investment in its completion to examine the poem with a perceptive eye when it is presented to them as an intact and authorized version. What, then, might they make of it? How is the poem as a whole to be interpreted?

The insertion which most obviously calls for explanation is the last. Why *snow*? Like the last line of the Edward Thomas poem, it fits in prosodically, in the pattern of metre and rhyme, but it seems somewhat incongruous, if not contradictory. How can the cherry tree be hung with bloom and with snow at the same time? Does Housman actually mean snow as such or is he talking metaphorically about something else? If we take the word *snow* in its literal sense as referring in the usual way there is a difficulty. But of course since it is in a poem it is not referring in the usual way. We need to look not for a literal but a literary significance. What might it be?

As we have already noticed, the two words *bloom* and *snow* appear in the same grammatical pattern *hung with* . . . in verses one and three. There is another pattern in verse one which is repeated in verse three, namely *about the* . . .; and it was this recurrence indeed which provided evidence for the filling of gap 3. Now in this second case, there was lexical repetition also (*woodland ride/woodlands*) so that the expressions are quite explicitly equivalent in meaning. But the patterning within these verses is such that it carries the implication that the words *bloom* and *snow*, worked in as parts of the pattern, are equivalent in meaning also. But how can they be when they are semantically so distinct: almost as distinct, one might say, as chalk and cheese? We have already noticed that they are alike in that they share the feature of whiteness, but apart from that their meanings are quite different.

But in what respects are they different? Let us consider what associations the two words invoke. *Bloom*: blossom, the flowering of trees, spring, and the emergence of new life. *Snow*: coldness, winter, and the abeyance of life. Life and death: two concepts in direct opposition. But are they in opposition? They take on the same appearance: they are both white. And the trees are wearing white, like clothing, like robes perhaps, for *Eastertide*. They are represented as celebrating not only the season of spring but the festival of Easter. What is the significance of this? Easter celebrates the resurrection of Christ after the crucifixion: death and life as mutually implied, the opposites mysteriously reconciled as one. We might suggest, then, that what these verses represent is the elusive but certain sense of the complex and complementary significance of life and death.

But this is not the only perspective represented in the poem. We come now to the second verse. Here, life and death are not complex at all. On the contrary, they are very straightforward, a matter of simple arithmetic calculation: you have your span of threescore years and ten, and if you have had twenty of these already, then you have only another fifty to go, and that's that. The reality represented in this second verse is in stark contrast to that represented in the first and last. Its very banality acts as an effective foil. And yet this too is part of the pattern and, though contrasting, is also congruent: the commonplace and the mysterious are somehow reconciled in the very patterns of language in the poem, the simplicity and regularity of which suggest something which is experienced as ordinary and superficial, and yet at the same time transcendental and profound.

But the experience is represented and not explicitly described. The meanings that can be read into the poem, therefore, are allusive, elusive, and implied, and cannot be pinned down by definitive interpretation. Some students might indeed dissent, demur at the meanings I have suggested and make the poem their own in different ways. They should feel free to do this, only on condition that they can provide reasons for their interpretation by reference to the text. What needs to be made clear is that this elusiveness of meaning is not, as it might be in other uses of language, a communicative defect that can be remedied, but an essential design feature of poetry as representation. 'The meaning escapes', to use Wallace Stevens's phrase; the poem 'will not declare itself', and its effect tends to diminish in inverse proportion to the extent to which it is 'certain as meaning'.

6 Intertextual comparison and the use of variants

We have now passed under brief review two kinds of procedure for getting students engaged with poetic texts: composition (in Chapter 4) and completion (in Chapter 5). I now want to consider a third: comparison. This is not only alliteratively related. It has to do with the intertextual associations which I discussed in the first part of this book (Chapter 9) and is designed to complement the textual and contextual procedures of composition and completion by extending student activity into the area of literary appreciation. We trespass here, of course, on to the terrain ceded by custom to literary criticism, but we are coming to it from a less familiar linguistic direction.

Intertextual comparison, then. One way of making students aware of the way meanings are exclusively yet elusively represented through the particular patterns of language in poetry, while necessarily at the same time developing their sensitivity to the subtleties of language in general, is to present them with an alternative text in parallel. This can be the rendering of the propositional content of the poem in question as a kind of intralingual poetic translation. Such alternative texts can be written so that the implied meanings that I have suggested can be read into a poem are more explicitly stated, and where the features referred to in proposing an interpretation are largely absent. The Housman poem, for example, might be reformulated as follows:

> The cherry is in bloom I see,
> It really is the loveliest tree.
> The snow-white blossom on the bough
> Tells me of life renewing now.

But my years don't renew, they die;
Twenty already have gone by,
Twenty that will not come again
Out of my three score years and ten.

So I must use these passing hours
To see spring come alive in flowers,
And look, before it is too late,
How things in spring regenerate.

Of course, being a poem (albeit not a very distinguished one) this is not certain as meaning either, and will also play host in some respects to variable response. But much of what was undeclared in the original poem, the implied meaning of the cherry blossom that was drawn out by interpretation, is here explicitly stated. And as this meaning is made certain, so it reduces in significance. At this point, we might use a comparison of these two poems, the authorized and derived versions, to discuss matters of relative artistic value, raising the issues of convergence and divergence (though not necessarily in these terms) that were discussed in the first half of this book. Thus it might be suggested that the derived version is, as verbal art, inferior to the authorized one precisely because it converges on a conclusion and makes its meaning plain. We might pursue this suggestion further by considering other reformulations which reduce the original to versions which are even more summary. For example:

The cherry tree
  Is blooming now,
With snow-white blossom
  On the bough.

I'm twenty years old,
  So I know
I have just fifty
  Years to go.

That's not much time
  For me to sing
About the blossom
  In the spring.

Or, more succinctly still:

> The cherry tree
>   Is blooming now
> With snow-white blossom
>   On the bough.
>
> There's not much time
>   For me to sing
> About the blossom
>   In the spring.

Reductions of this kind inevitably diminish the effects of the original, and part of their purpose is, of course, to draw attention to this. But they can also create different effects of their own. Reduction can result in explicitness, which narrows down interpretative possibilities. But it can also result in reticence, which allows for a wider range of interpretation. I will be returning to the different effects of poetic reduction in a later chapter.

So far in this chapter we have been dealing with derived versions. An intertexual comparison might also be made between the original poem by A.E. Housman and the one by Edward Thomas discussed previously. In both of them we find a fusion of the commonplace and the transcendental, the reconciliation of two apparently opposing perspectives on reality. We might see them as variations on a theme. They are, of course, also alike in that they both deal with transition from one stage of time to another: from day to night on the one hand, from winter to spring on the other. This suggests a possible principle of selection: the grouping of poems which are comparable in respect to common thematic import. By reference to this principle, we can also associate the Thomas poem with others which have to do with the smaller temporal scale of the dawn and the resumption of life after the dark, and the Housman poem with others which express the larger temporal scale of the seasons and the renewal of life after the winter.

In the case of Edward Thomas's *Cock-Crow*, for example, we might invite students to consider Browning's song from *Pippa Passes*, which was discussed in the first part of this book. Another possibility might be Isaac Rosenberg's poem *Returning, We Hear the Larks*. Here the experience of daybreak is represented very differently and the singing of the lark, rejected as an irrelevant distraction in the Thomas poem, takes on a particularly poignant significance. And since the poem deals with life and death, it is thematically related also to the Housman poem.

Returning, We Hear the Larks

Sombre the night is:
And, though we have our lives, we know
What sinister threat lurks there.

Dragging these anguished limbs, we only know
This poison-blasted track opens on our camp—
On a little safe sleep.

But hark! Joy—joy—strange joy.
Lo! Heights of night ringing with unseen larks:
Music showering on our upturned listening faces.

Death could drop from the dark
As easily as song—
But song only dropped,
Like a blind man's dreams on the sand
By dangerous tides;
Like a girl's dark hair, for she dreams no ruin lies there,
Or her kisses where a serpent hides.

As before, it might be appropriate for students to be initially drawn into the poem by the kind of composition or completion activities that were demonstrated in the preceding chapters. And appreciation of the literary effect of particular features of its language can, again as before, be prompted by a comparison with a rewritten version. Here is an example:

The night is dark and sombre; though
We have our lives still, we all know
A sinister threat lurks in the night.

We, dragging anquished limbs, go back
Along the poison-blasted track
To find safe sleep, a brief respite.

But then strange joy comes from the dark,
From heights of night we hear the lark,
Showering music from the air.

Death could drop from darkness so,
As easily as song, but no,
It's only singing that falls there.

Singing like a blind man's dreams
On the sand by dangerous tides,
Or like a girl's dark hair it seems,
Or kisses where a serpent hides.

This version retains much of the original and differs mainly in its prosodic patterning, the introduction of rhyme and metrical regularity. The question to be considered is what effect such reshaping has in the way in which the experience is represented. But we could, of course, make greater changes and produce a more radically different version. This might take the form of a simpler poetic reformulation of what seems to be the main theme of the original. In this case, the comparison would draw more attention to the effect of the images in the original text (*poison-blasted track*, for example, *blind man's dreams*, *girl's dark hair*) which are absent from the derived version. Here is one possibility:

Escaped from death, the troops came, tired and worn,
Returning to their hard-earned rest at dawn.

And in the silence as they marched along,
They heard the music of a skylark's song.

They turned their eyes to heaven at this singing,
As if in hope a new life was beginning.

In the case of Housman, we might invite comparison with Philip Larkin's poem *The Trees*, which also relates seasonal change to a sense of renewal, and to 'something almost being said' about the inexplicable experience of, so to speak, the resurrection and the life. Whether students are to first participate in the assembly of the poem along the lines already suggested, or whether it is to be presented for comparison in its complete authorized form is a matter of local pedagogic decision. It will depend on who the students are and where they are in respect to linguistic competence and literary understanding. This is the authorized Larkin version:

The trees are coming into leaf
Like something almost being said;
The recent buds relax and spread,
Their greenness is a kind of grief.

Is it that they are born again
And we grow old? No, they die too.
Their yearly trick of looking new
Is written down in rings of grain.

Yet still the unresting castles thresh
In fullgrown thickness every May.
Last year is dead, they seem to say,
Begin afresh, afresh, afresh.

In this case we might vary procedure a little and provide a less radically changed alternative version for critical comparison: here we
just transpose the lines and make relatively minor adjustments to
the syntax. In general, of course, the smaller the differences between the original and its derivation, the more demands are made
on the students' critical perception to discover their significance.
So the degree and type of textual alteration can serve to regulate
difficulty of task and thus guide and monitor the gradual development of literary appreciation.

Like something almost being said,
The recent buds relax and spread;
Their greenness is a kind of grief.
The trees are coming into leaf.

We age and they are born again.
Not so, for there in rings of grain,
Their yearly trick of looking new
Is written down. No, they die too.

In fullgrown thickness every May,
Last year is dead, they seem to say.
Yet still the unresting castles thresh.
Begin afresh, afresh, afresh.

What I am suggesting, then, is that intertextual comparisons can
be made between different authorized texts on the one hand, and
between authorized texts and derived versions on the other. In the
first case, this leads to a selection and grouping of poems for treatment which are thematically related in some way. The relationship can, of course, be more or less evident. One might bring
together poems whose propositional content is clearly comparable in terms of their referential paraphrases: poems which are
'about' the same thing, which are topically alike. Thus we could

group together poems about particular actualities or abstractions (often indicated by title): animals, birds, trees and flowers, cities and seasons, war and peace, love, loneliness, absence, bereavement, and so on. But one might also wish to juxtapose poems whose thematic links are less obvious and which are more a matter of what they are interpreted as representing through propositional content which is superficially quite different. There is of course the difficulty that such covert associations are of their nature a function of particular interpretations, and one has to guard against the danger of pre-empting student response by implying a connection in advance. On the other hand, the juxtaposition of poems which on one interpretation at least can be read as thematically related can act as a challenge. There is no reason why students should accept the implied connection. If they reject it in preference to a different interpretation for which they can invoke textual evidence, so much the better.

There is, however, a further difficulty about thematic content in general which is less easy to resolve. It is that students may not be able to access the significance of a poem, in part or whole, quite simply because it presupposes knowledge, beliefs, attitudes which characterize a culture other than their own and which they are unaware of or cannot share. An obvious instance of this is the significance of heraldry and Eastertide in the Thomas and Housman poems we considered earlier. Perhaps the first thing that needs to be noted is that such cultural problems are all-pervasive. And they are bound to be, since the writers of poetry, and indeed of literature in general, make their representations out of the language and culture current in their own community. And these obviously change in the same place over time as much as they vary in different places at the same time. So the problem of cultural content in poems in English is not by any means unique to those for whom English is a foreign language. English-speaking students will have to grapple with all manner of unfamiliar assumptions and allusions in the literature of an earlier period, even one which is relatively recent, and in the literature of a different social class or community, even one which is contemporary with their own. And sometimes there are surprising congruences, where the present culture of one community seems in some respects and at some level to key in with the past culture of another. But we cannot, of course, count on such congruence. What, then, do we do about unshared background knowledge, about unfamiliar conventions of thought and behaviour, about such things as seasonal change, war on the Western Front, cherry trees in bloom, larks on the wing, heraldry and Eastertide, and all other culturally specific expressions of human experience? How, in general, are we to cope with this problem of obscure cultural content?

There are, I think, two points to be made. Firstly (and here I rehearse an argument of the first part of this book), there is always some disparity of realities in human communication of any kind. The meanings we achieve are always approximate and never complete. In other discourses, we are generally expected to converge as closely as possible on a common purpose. In literary discourses, this expectation is relaxed and we are free to diverge. We are not under the same social pressure to come to a conclusion. So even if certain allusions are lost on readers, this does not prevent them from making meaning out of the text in relation to their own realities. In a sense, learning to read poetry is the discovery of significance without certainty. So interpreting a poem does not, and indeed cannot, depend on the knowledge of cultural allusions, or of the individual or social circumstances of its composition. What a poem means is what it means to its readers. They make it their own.

At the same time, an increase in this cultural and circumstantial knowledge naturally increases what I have called *poetentiality*, that is to say, the potential of the poetic text to activate a wider range of possible interpretations. And this brings me to my second point. Once the students' interest in a poem is engaged, and they are encouraged into individual response, there is a likelihood that those problematic aspects which they cannot incorporate into their interpretations will act as a stimulus to their curiosity, and they will seek out their significance. This can be done initially through dictionary reference. Subsequently, further encyclopedic information can be provided, as required, by the teacher or some other source. The essential point is that the information is not given in advance as a prerequisite but as part of the process of enquiry into the poem's meanings. It is not a precondition but a consequence of interpretation. So a lack of cultural knowledge need not be seen as a negative factor but, on the contrary, as something that can be turned to positive advantage.

And this advantage is twofold. Firstly, as I have just suggested, this discovery procedure can develop an awareness that poetry admits of a range of meanings, and so contribute to literary appreciation. Secondly, it can provide the means whereby students, on their own initiative, acquire information about conventional realities other than their own. In this respect, the reading of poetry serves the cause of cross-cultural understanding. In short, I am making the bold claim that the approach that I am outlining here can bring the concerns of language, literature, and culture into an intimate and integral relationship.

7 Comparing poems with prose description

In the preceding chapter I demonstrated the activity of intertextual comparison only by reference to poetic texts. But comparison can also be made between passages of prose and poems which represent the same or similar propositional content. I offered one example of this earlier (in Chapter 5 of Part One) when I discussed in some detail the difference between the way events were referred to by Dorothy Wordsworth in her journal and the way her brother William represented them in his poem. The demonstration and discussion of this particular pair of texts might be taken as a model for a more general pedagogic activity whereby referential descriptions of phenomena and events are compared with poems which represent them in different ways.

Although authorized texts as closely parallel as these Wordsworth ones are relatively rare, it is not difficult to find those of sufficient similarity of content for revealing comparisons to be made. The factual descriptions of flora and fauna to be found in encyclopedia entries, for example, can serve as points of reference for innumerable poetic treatments of such subjects. Cherry trees and chestnut trees, yew trees and birches, lilies, roses, daffodils, the woodspurge and the lesser celandine; skylarks, cuckoos, crows, hawks, horses and foxes, the snake and the tiger, fireflies and dragonflies, and the cabbage white: all the botanical variety and the menagerie of creatures great and small that figure, in central or supporting roles, in poetry can be comparatively considered, reference against representation.

With this in mind, consider, as an example of reference, the following text, descriptive of the (sky)lark taken from the *Collins Pocket Guide to British Birds*:

SKYLARK   *Alauda arvensis*

PLUMAGE.   Brown, streaked darker and paler beneath; a noticeable crest at times; white feathers in tail. Thin horn-coloured bill; yellowish-brown legs.

MOVEMENT.   Flight rather undulating; walks.

VOICE.   Flight- and call-note a liquid 'chirrup'; sustained, warbling song is normally delivered in the air, but sometimes on ground and even from a perch. The only bird which habitually sings while ascending almost vertically, while hovering in the air (often nearly out of sight) and again while descending almost vertically.

FIELD MARKS.   Can confidently be identified by song habits alone.

FLOCKING.   Very gregarious after breeding, especially on migration and in hard weather.

HABITAT.   Exclusively open country.

We may now set this text alongside poetic texts (among them that of Rosenberg previously cited) and consider how they compare. For example:

But hark! Joy—joy—strange joy.
Lo! Heights of night ringing with unseen larks:
Music showering on our upturned listening faces.
(Rosenberg: *Returning, We Hear the Larks*)

Haply I think on thee — and then my state,
Like to the lark at break of day arising
From sullen earth, sings hymns at heaven's gate.
(Shakespeare: *Sonnets, 29*)

Hail to thee, blithe spirit!
　Bird thou never wert,
That from heaven or near it
　Pourest thy full heart
In profuse strains of unpremeditated art.

Higher still and higher
　From the earth thou springest,
Like a cloud of fire;
　The blue deep thou wingest,
And singing still dost soar, and soaring ever singest.
(Shelley: *To a Skylark*)

Ethereal minstrel! pilgrim of the sky!
Dost thou despise the earth where cares abound?
Or, while the wings aspire, are heart and eye
Both with thy nest upon the dewy ground?
Thy nest which thou canst drop into at will,
Those quivering wings composed, that music still!

Leave to the nightingale her shady wood;
A privacy of glorious light is thine;
Whence thou dost pour upon the world a flood
Of harmony, with instinct more divine;
Type of the wise who soar, but never roam;
True to the kindred points of Heaven and Home!
(Wordsworth: *To the Skylark*)

And drowned in yonder living blue
The lark becomes a sightless song.
(Tennyson: *In Memoriam*)

We may begin (as we did with the Wordsworth texts) by asking students to note which features of this bird, comprehensively detailed in the referential description, are singled out as significant for representation. In none of these lines is there any mention of plumage. The crest may be noticeable but it is not considered to be poetically noteworthy. Nothing is said of its habitat, nor of the fact that it walks rather than hops along the ground. The poetic texts only correspond with the guide book description in respect to the features which come under the heading of *Voice*. Even here, what is seen to be relevant is not the liquid 'chirrup', nor the fact that the sustained warbling, though normally delivered in flight, can also be produced on the ground or when perching. What the poetic texts focus their attention on almost entirely is the fact that the lark sings as it ascends and descends and while hovering in the air, often almost invisible. Now why should this be so?

Well, we are told that the skylark is the only bird that habitually behaves in this way, so it is not surprising that poets should fix upon this distinctive feature. But what do they make of it? They do not just say that the bird sings while ascending and descending and hovering in the air. They represent this as an opposition between heaven and earth, the spiritual and the ordinary, the inspired and the dull. The bird rises in flight and song and then disappears into the glorious light of the empyrean. It becomes an ethereal minstrel, its singing and soaring become one, its sightless song is a hymn at heaven's gate, unseen and on high it becomes disembodied, a divine instinct and a blithe spirit. The lark is transmogrified. The referential facts about its habitual behaviour have been converted into a representation of spiritual life freeing itself first from the earth in flight, and then from the body in song. And this is associated, appropriately enough, with the dawn. The fact that the lark's song is a feature of the early day is not mentioned at all in the guide book. This is because it is not relevant to the description since it does not distinguish the lark from other birds: they all start singing early in the morning. It is simply that the lark's habit of doing it hovering in the air makes it more noticeable. This feature of behaviour is, however, made relevant in the poetry.

So this intertextual comparison can help to bring home to students, through guided discussion, the differences in general between conventional and poetic modes of meaning. This could provide the basis for further developments. We might, for example, go on to consider how other features of the bird referred to in the guide book description might be poeticized. One might notice the marked contrast between what it sounds like and what it looks like, between its unremarkable appearance on the ground and its remarkable singing in the air. Can we make a poem out of these features which gives significance to the contrast? Students can be invited to try, and given whatever guidance seems appropriate. They might have their attention drawn to certain details out of the descriptive text: details like *brown plumage, white-feathered tail, crest, open country, hovering in the air*, and so on; then perhaps be provided with a selection of other words and phrases and an opening line to get them started:

Skylark. What glorious notes it sings.

Or, following the procedures previously illustrated, they might be given a set of lines to compose or complete. Or they might simply be presented with a poem, already composed and complete and incorporating the contrast in question, for them to subject to comparative consideration. The following, for example:

Skylark. What glorious notes it sings,
Hovering in the air above its nest,
So high you cannot see its wings,
Its tail, white-feathered, or its crest.

The open country all around
Rings with the singing from its throat.
And then it drops down to the ground:
A dull brown bird of little note.

An alternative (or additional) development would be into literary criticism of a more familiar kind by way of a comparison between complete authorized poetic texts, between Wordsworth's poem on the skylark, for example, and Shelley's (one on *the* skylark, we should note; the other on *a* skylark). The preceding activities, I would argue, will have helped to prime students to perceive the differences: Shelley's skylark, an insubstantial spirit soaring to the heavens, and released from earthly connections completely; Wordsworth's soaring, but not roaming, ethereal but also down to earth. And so on, each poem expressing a different vision of reality.

But enough now of skylarks and the *Collins Pocket Guide to British Birds*. There are of course many other types of text, apart from the encyclopedic kind, which can be used for such intertextual comparison. Consider again the poem by Isaac Rosenberg. So far we have treated it as a poem about larks and have set it alongside other texts on the same topic. But it is also, of course, about war, about the fear and fatigue of soldiers as they return from fighting to the relative security of their camp: indeed it is the incongruous association of the larks singing with what usually comes out of the sky on the battlefield, of joy with death, that gives point and poignancy to the poem. To sharpen perception of how the experience of war is expressed in such poetry, we can set it alongside referential accounts of different kinds: those, for example, of journalists, historians, and soldiers themselves. The following three texts deal with war (more specifically with the Third Battle of Ypres, Passchendaele, 1917) at different degrees of distance from the actuality of the battlefield.[13]

Text 1

The Times, 23 August 1917
Successful operations were undertaken by our troops this morning, east and north-east of Ypres, for the capture of a series of strongpoints and fortified farms lying a few hundred yards in front of our positions astride the Ypres–Menin Road and between the Ypres–Roulers railway and Langemarck.

Bitter fighting has taken place at all points. The enemy has again launched repeated counter-attacks which have suffered heavy losses from our artillery and machine-gun fire.

Text 2

It was a costly exercise. The strongpoints of Beck and Borry were still undefeated. The infantry had not been able to advance by so much as an inch the line that ran between Square Farm and Low Farm. Their ranks were horribly depleted, while, in the blood-soaked field beyond, some hundreds more men had dropped to swell the ranks of the dead. The results of this minor action were regarded at Headquarters as being disappointing. It was noted with regret that two companies of the Argyll and Sutherland Highlanders had lost all their officers, and that over 200 other ranks were killed, wounded or missing.

Text 3

Lieutenant Burns said to me, 'You'd better get a message back, Morgan, and let them know what's happening. We must have reinforcements.'

We were standing in this wet shell-hole and he was just handing me the message when the machine-gun bullet got him. He fell right over on to me and we both went right down into the water. I managed to pull him a bit up the side of this crater and laid him down and knelt down beside him. His eyes were open and he looked straight up at me and he said, 'I'm all right, Mum.' And then he died. He was younger than me. I was twenty.

We might consider first the differences between these referential texts. To begin with, it might be observed (as indicated earlier) that there is a progressive narrowing of focus in description, a coming into close-up, so to speak. Locations become more precise: Text 1 gives general map references and talks about indefinite strongpoints and fortified farms. In Text 2 these are named (*Beck* and *Borry, Square Farm* and *Low Farm*). In Text 3, location is specific and immediate in proximity (*this wet shell-hole, this crater*). Consistent with this narrowing of focus on location there is an increase in specificity of reference to the participants involved. We just have *troops* in Text 1. In Text 2 we have *infantry, men, companies of Argyll and Sutherland Highlanders, officers*, and *other ranks*: we seem to be getting closer to actual people. And in Text 3, we have particular individuals: *Lieutenant Burns, Morgan*. And with this increased focus on people comes quite naturally a change in the way their fate is described. In Text 1, it is only the enemy that has losses, and the word *death* is not mentioned. In Text 2, soldiers quite explicitly die, and in great numbers: *to swell the ranks of the dead*. In Text 3 the death of a particular human being is described in detail: the indefinite *machine-gun fire* of Text 1 has become very definitely and fatally *the machine-gun bullet* in Text 3. And as we move towards particulars in place and person, so there is a growing authorial involvement in what is reported. Texts 1 and 2 are both third-person descriptions. The former, however, reveals no attitudinal commitment of any kind. The events are recounted in detachment. There are in Text 2, on the other hand, expressions of an evaluative kind like *horribly depleted* and *blood-soaked field* which suggest emotional involvement; and the way the reactions of Headquarters are referred to, with the use of the expressions *minor action* and *disappointing*, sounds ironical. Text 3, of course, is a first-person narrative of personal experience.

At this point, we can introduce a poetic text for comparison. A considerable number of poems have been written about the First World War by those who had direct experience of it. Two poets indeed have written prose accounts as well (Robert Graves: *Goodbye to All That*; Siegfried Sassoon: *Memoirs of an Infantry Officer*) and these provide an admirable source of comparable texts. But as illustration of the present procedure (I shall come back to Sassoon in the next chapter) the following will serve our purpose. It is (part of) a poem by Wilfred Owen. It perhaps has its own particular appropriacy. Owen was, like Lieutenant Burns, killed in action. Furthermore, his poem is comparable with that by Rosenberg, in that it, too, is about soldiers dragging their anguished limbs, returning from the front. Only this time, it is indeed death, and not lark song which drops upon them.

Dulce et Decorum Est

Bent double, like old beggars under sacks,
Knock-kneed, coughing like hags, we cursed through sludge,
Till on the haunting flares we turned our backs,
And towards our distant rest began to trudge.
Men marched asleep. Many had lost their boots,
But limped on, blood-shod. All went lame, all blind;
Drunk with fatigue; deaf even to the hoots
Of gas-shells dropping softly behind.

Gas! Gas! Quick, boys!—An ecstasy of fumbling,
Fitting the clumsy helmets just in time,
But someone still was yelling out and stumbling
And floundering like a man in fire or lime.—
Dim through the misty panes and thick green light,
As under a green sea, I saw him drowning.

In all my dreams before my helpless sight
He plunges at me, guttering, choking, drowning . . .

To which of the three prose passages does this one most closely
correspond? Clearly Text 3. Here, too, we have a first-person account (*we*, not *they*, *cursed through sludge*, etc.). We have the
same expression of immediate experience: actual words are
recorded in both (*Gas! Gas! Quick, boys!*) and the definite article
in both implies an immediacy of context (compare *the machine-
gun bullet* in Text 3 and *the haunting flares* in the poem). In both
prose text and poem we have the witnessing of an individual
death. Are they, then, accounts of the same sort? How are the
deaths actually described? In Text 3, the facts are baldly stated,
events appear in the straightforward sequence of their occurrence
linked up by the co-ordinate conjunction *and*: this happened and
then this happened and then this. The verbs which describe the
events are plain, minimally descriptive: *He fell right over on to
me, we both went right down, I managed to pull him up a bit, laid
him down*. There is no stumbling or floundering here. The noun
phrases are uniformly simple: the only modification that occurs is
the word *wet*. This starkly factual description is in marked contrast to the verbal elaboration of the poem. Here the description
of the event is loaded down with detail. The men are not just going

back to camp, they are *cursing through sludge*, they are *trudging, limping, stumbling, bent double, knock-kneed, lame*, and so on. The present participles, which are so thickly distributed throughout the poem (compare, again, the prevalence of the simple tense in the prose text), themselves carry the grammatical meaning of duration. And all of the detail of suffering and fatigue in the first verse, expressed through the heavily charged descriptive phrases that clog up the syntactic development is itself like an encumbrance, weighing upon them, slowing them down. So much so, we might suggest, that when the emergency comes, as it does, patterned in the verse to be a part of their exhaustion, the reaction to it is inevitably slow and clumsy. *Gas! Gas! Quick, boys!* But they cannot be quick: the language again, both grammar and lexis, expresses their clumsy movements, their fumbling and stumbling. What experience, it might be asked, is this suggestive of? Where do we have this agonizing experience of needing to move quickly and urgently but having to drag our limbs along like lead? In dreams, surely. And is this not what we have here: not the report of an event, as we have in Text 3, but the *representation* of the event experienced as a nightmare? Hence, we might suggest, the appropriateness of the phrase *the haunting flares* in verse 1, and the dimness, the *misty panes, the thick green light* in verse 2. And, of course, dreams are explicitly mentioned in the third verse, with their familiar sense of helplessness, and where the elusive, dreamlike experience of timelessly present duration is captured in the three present participles: *guttering, choking, drowning*.

We might explore other aspects of the poem as providing evidence of such representational effects. We might note, for example, that the actual words that occur at the beginning of verse 2 are not, as they are in Text 3, recorded as direct speech: there is no sign of the conventional inverted commas. Why not? We might note, too, that although the poem can be said to express individual experience, it is also strangely general, and lacking in specificity. Indeed, as a factual account, it does not ring true at all. *Men marched asleep. All* of them? And how **can** they be asleep while they are marching? *All went lame, all blind. All?* Surely not. And are all the soldiers bent double, all knock-kneed, all coughing like hags? They obviously could not have been in actual reality. All this overstatement would be out of place in factual reference, of the kind we find in the prose text. But this is not reference, it is representation. And all these features of the poem are appropriate to a nightmare vision of the event which, we might argue, is what Owen is seeking to describe. As before, then, comparison provides the starting point, but once activated, critical enquiry into the significance of the poem's language can take on its own momentum. And, again as before, the students can be presented with, or be guided towards composing, derived versions which help to give further focus to the features of the original. Here, to end this chapter, is one possibility:

> We struggled on, footsore and worn,
> Returning to our rest at dawn,
> Lame and tired and almost blind.
> Then softly gas-shells dropped behind.
>
> Fumbling to put helmets on,
> All managed just in time, save one:
> I saw him choke in thick green light,
> Drowning in death before my sight.

8 Deriving poems from prose description

The intertextual comparison demonstrated in Chapter 7 dealt with the relationship between different authorized texts of prose and poetry. At one point, however, I suggested that, as a follow-up exercise, students might consider how poetry (about the skylark in this case) can be derived by using details from a prose source other than those appearing in the poems to be compared. In this chapter I want to develop this line a little further. Here, then, our main interest is in the process of direct poetic derivation from a passage of authorized prose. The idea, again, is that such derivation can help students to appreciate the distinctive nature of poetry and the kind of reading that it calls for in the interpretation of its significance.

As examples, I want to consider two passages from the writing of Siegfried Sassoon. These continue the war theme introduced in the preceding chapter, and, like the poem by Rosenberg, set the violence of conflict in a context of the normal and natural world. In the first of them, even the lark makes its (by now) familiar appearance. An advantage of selecting from Sassoon's prose is that the poetic derivations can be subsequently set alongside original poems which Sassoon wrote himself, so we can follow the comparative sequence: authorized prose—derived poem—authorized poem. Here is the first passage:

> *Wednesday 6.15 p.m. On Crawley Ridge.* Very still evening; sun rather hazy. Looking across to Fricourt; trench mortars bursting in the cemetery; dull white smoke slowly floats away over grey-green grass with buttercups and saffron weeds. Fricourt; a huddle of reddish roofs; skeleton village; church tower, almost demolished, a white patch against green of Fricourt wood (full of German batteries). North, up the hill, white seams and heapings of trenches dug in chalk. Sky full of

lark songs. Sometimes you can count thirty slowly and hear no sound of a shot; then the muffled pop of a rifle or a slamming 5.9 or one of our 18-pounders. Then a burst of machine-gun fire. Westward the yellow sky with a web of filmy cloud half across the sun; the ridges with blurred outlines of trees. An aeroplane droning overhead. A thistle sprouting through the chalk on the parapet; a cockchafer sailing through the air.
(Memoirs of an Infantry Officer)

The first activity might be to make a selection of details from this description and then to get discussion going as to how these might be incorporated into a poetic version. This can be seen as a more demanding variant of the assembling activity that was demonstrated earlier (in Chapter 4). How, then, might we compose a poem out of the following expressions, using extra language to make a fit where necessary? Some of the given expressions are reformulated phrases, and some direct citations from the passage:

the evening still / sun hazy at this hour / smoke floating / dull white / the cemetery / village / red roofs / half-demolished tower / white shape against the green / grass and tree / westward the yellow sky / a web of filmy cloud / the sun / sky full of lark songs / time passes by / the muffled firing of a gun / machine-gun fire / mortars burst out there / an aeroplane drones overhead / a thistle is sprouting on the parapet / a cockchafer comes sailing through the air.

One can, of course, set different conditions on composition, and these will be constraints for some students, which will make the task more problematic, and guidance for others, which will make the task easier. We could, for example, require regularity of pattern in metrical rhythm and rhyme scheme, or alternatively allow free verse. We could provide frameworks: the outline pattern of the verse form with opening lines provided, or with the rhyming words in place. The activity can obviously be adapted to suit the purposes, linguistic and literary, of different groups of students. In some situations, it will be appropriate to work with students towards a particular version, assembled in advance. At all events, whatever pedagogic tactics are used, the teacher would probably prefer to base them on a derived text previously prepared. Here is the derived poem that served as such a basis in the present case.

On Crawley Ridge

The evening still. Sun hazy at this hour.
Smoke floating, dull white, from the cemetery.
Village. Red roofs and half-demolished tower,
White shape against the green of grass and tree.

The evening still. Westward the yellow sky.
A web of filmy cloud across the sun.
Sky full of lark songs. And time passes by
Between the muffled firing of a gun.

Machine-gun fire and mortars burst out there.
An aeroplane drones overhead. And yet,
A cockchafer comes sailing through the air,
A thistle's sprouting on the parapet.

The next move is to consider the effects of this poeticization: what are the distinctive features of the poem and what do we read into them which we do not read into the original prose description? In both cases, it might be remarked, the perceptions of sights and sounds are recorded as sets of notes, for the most part as a series of grammatically unconnected noun phrases. But in the poem these are arranged in the patterning of prosodic form: the regularity of rhythm and rhyme suggest not just random observation but some underlying order, some completed and coherent shape to what is perceived. This can be said to be confirmed by the last two sentences, which are structurally parallel, and where, for the only time in the poem, the grammatical and prosodic patterns converge: the syntax in each case is complete and contained within the metrical line. These are not just random notes. There is an effect of closure and completion. What, we might wonder, is the possible significance of this? Well, perhaps we are making too much of the occurrence of a couple of sentences. There are sentences in the original prose text as well after all. Are there? In fact, there are not many. Indeed, sentences with finite verbs only occur twice in all, and in different parts of the passage (*dull white smoke slowly floats . . ., you can count . . .*). The rest of the text consists entirely of noun phrases (over twenty of them). What of the poem? It might be observed at this point that in the first half we find noun phrases and *only* noun phrases: there is not a sentence in sight. Then, in the second half these unattached phrases disappear entirely and we have only syntactically complete sentences. The

expression *And time passes by* marks the transition. What are we ·
to make of this? The scene up to this point is static, but now as
time starts up again, it takes on movement. Things do not just
exist, they happen. There is activity: mortars burst, an aeroplane
drones. War returns. But then, life resumes as well: a cockchafer
comes sailing through the air and a thistle is sprouting—
sprouting, we might note, on the very parapet of the trench. And
this resumption of life, in spite of the destruction of war, is
expressed through verb forms which are not only finite, but continuous. It is durative, and so, we might suggest, it endures; especially since it is this which is expressed as a closure within the
particularly marked patterning of language in these last two lines
which we have already noted.

The version we have been considering keeps very close to the
referential text. But, as I suggested earlier, we could alter the conditions for derivation thus allowing for the possibility of very different variants, which might then be compared. Or students could
be presented with an alternative derivation, and then guided into
a comparison with the one we have been considering. For
example:

The sun is hazy at this hour.
White smoke floats from the cemetery.
Against the green of grass and tree,
Rises the white ruin of the tower.

A web of cloud across the sun
Hangs in the yellow western sky,
And, as larks sing, time passes by
In the muffled firing of a gun.

The sound of warfare beats out there,
An aeroplane drones by. And yet
A thistle on the parapet
Grows up and reaches for the air.

Let us now consider the second Sassoon passage. We can perhaps
illustrate here one of the variations of the activity that I suggested
before and present students with the prose text together with a
verse framework within which it is to be reassembled, consisting
of a number of completed and uncompleted lines and a rhyme
scheme, giving no other guidance (except perhaps a title). Such
an activity is, in reference to those discussed earlier, in part

composition and in part completion. Here is the passage:

> Ploughmen with their grey teams drove a last furrow on the skyline; windmills spun their sails merrily; rooks came cawing home from the fields; pigeons circled above farmstead stacks with whistling sober-hued wings; and the old shepherd drove his sheep and goats into the village tootling on a pipe. Sometimes a rampart of approaching rain would blot out the distance, but the foreground would be striped with vivid green, lit with a gleam of sun, and an arc of iridescence spanned the slate-coloured cloud. The War was fifty kilometres away, though we could hear the big guns booming beyond the horizon.
> *(Memoirs of a Fox-hunting Man)*

And here is (one) verse framework:

Approaching Storm

On the skyline, ploughmen with their teams

_____ they would do that day;

_____ around,

_____ their homeward way.

Into the village, the shepherd drove his herd,

_____ a tune or two;

_____ stacks,

_____ of sober hue.

Sometimes a rampart of approaching rain

_____ but closer by,

_____ green;

_____ the sky.

_____ the slate-coloured cloud,
Making a strip of brightness in the gloom.

_____ , far away.

_____ boom.

I will present the completed poem (as I have assembled it) a little later. Meanwhile readers might wish to try completing it for themselves, and then, along the lines of the previous example, reflect on what is distinctive and significant about the derivation.

Deriving poems from these particular passages might be regarded as a relatively straightforward matter. Many of the phrases can be taken ready-made out of the prose and simply fitted into patterns to make the poem. Sassoon was, after all, a poet, and his prose, we might suggest, reflects the fact, has more potential poetic substance to it, so to speak, than would be the case with other texts. But all referential texts are, I would claim, open to representational reworking along these lines. There is no intrinsically poetic substance. Consider, for example, Text 2 in the preceding chapter. This looks to be unpromising material, but with a little ingenuity in the selection and shaping of phrase a poem can be derived from it. Here is the text again:

> It was a costly exercise. The strongpoints of Beck and Borry were still undefeated. The infantry had not been able to advance by so much as an inch the line that ran between Square Farm and Low Farm. Their ranks were horribly depleted, while, in the blood-soaked field beyond, some hundreds more men had dropped to swell the ranks of the dead. The results of this minor action were regarded at Headquarters as being disappointing. It was noted with regret that two companies of the Argyll and Sutherland Highlanders had lost all their officers, and that over 200 other ranks were killed, wounded or missing.

As was suggested earlier, there seems to be a certain degree of subjectivity here, of authorial involvement in the description. Considering the passage more closely, we might discern two perspectives on the events. One of them sees the human side of the fighting: the exercise is costly in terms of actual suffering, and this is expressed in phrases like *horribly depleted, blood-soaked field, the ranks of the dead*. The other perspective is that of the Headquarters staff, who see this event as a failure to achieve the plan of attack, and the exercise is costly in terms of statistics: this is expressed in phrases like *the results of this minor action, disappointing, it was noted with regret*. We might, then, begin a poem with the opening sentence of the text: *It was a costly exercise* and then try to represent this contrast of perspective by focusing on these phrases, thereby bringing out the irony which, I suggested earlier, could be read into the prose account. For example:

A Costly Exercise

It was a costly exercise.
Their strongpoints undefeated,
Our infantry was stopped,
And could not move ahead.
In the blood-soaked field, before my eyes,
Some hundreds more men dropped.
Their ranks were horribly depleted
To swell the ranks of dead.

A matter for dissatisfaction.
With no advance reported,
Headquarters quite upset.
Such losses in a minor action
Were noted with regret.

Not a very impressive poem perhaps, but a poem none the less, and as such can, as before, be compared with the prose text from which it is derived with a view to developing an awareness of the effects of such poetic reformulation.

These activities can (if desired) serve to prepare students for a consideration of authorized poems by Sassoon. Some of these deal with the contrast which we read into his prose passages, and represented in the poetic derivations, between the realities of war and normal, natural life, between the horror and the beauty. Alongside our second derivation (presented earlier as incomplete), we might set one of these poems and invite critical comparison.

Approaching Storm

On the skyline, ploughmen with their teams
Drove the last furrow they would do that day;
Merrily windmills spun their sails around,
And cawing rooks went on their homeward way.

Into the village, the shepherd drove his herd,
Tootling on a pipe a tune or two;
And pigeons circled above farmstead stacks,
Flying with whistling wings of sober hue.

Sometimes a rampart of approaching rain
Would blot the distance out, but closer by,
The foreground was all striped with vivid green,
An arc of iridescence spanned the sky.

A gleam of sun lit the slate-coloured cloud,
Making a strip of brightness in the gloom.
The war was in the distance, far away.
Beyond the horizon we could hear the big guns boom.

Everyone Sang

Everyone suddenly burst out singing;
And I was filled with such delight
As prisoned birds must find in freedom,
Winging wildly across the white
Orchards and dark-green fields; on—on—and out of sight.

Everyone's voice was suddenly lifted;
And beauty came like the setting sun:
My heart was shaken with tears; and horror
Drifted away . . . O, but Everyone
Was a bird; and the song was wordless; the singing will never
    be done.

A second theme which runs through much of Sassoon's poetry is
the contrasting perspectives on war, which were represented in
the modest verse derivation from Text 2 which was offered
earlier: the contrast between the suffering of soldiers at the front,
and the complacency of the staff at the base. This finds expression
in poems of bitter irony. The following is an example:

Base Details

If I were fierce, and bald, and short of breath,
I'd live with scarlet Majors at the Base,
And speed glum heroes up the line to death.
You'd see me with my puffy petulant face,
Guzzling and gulping in the best hotel,
Reading the Roll of Honour. 'Poor young chap,'
I'd say—'I used to know his father well;
Yes, we've lost heavily in this last scrap.'
And when the war is done and youth stone dead,
I'd toddle safely home and die—in bed.

Again, this authorized poem can be set alongside the derived poem *A Costly Exercise* for the purpose of critical comparison.

9   Deriving and comparing poetic variants

It might at this point be as well to give a brief reminder of the basic rationale behind the suggestions for practical classroom work that I have been making. The activities of textual recasting and comparison which have been proposed in the preceding chapters are intended to sharpen student perception of the ways language can be used to express different aspects of reality. The lesson to be learnt here (with respect to the general educational purpose discussed earlier) is that none of these aspects has any absolute legitimacy, but all are expressive of conditional truth and dependent on different perpectives and attitudes. It is easy to see that this point could be further elaborated by the kind of comparison of referential prose passages which was briefly undertaken with the three texts in Chapter 7. Indeed it might in some situations be appropriate to give primary attention to such texts, and bring in poetry only in a contingent and supporting role.

But in this book poetry is at the centre of things. The main purpose of the proposed activities is to get students to explore what the significance might be of poetic expressions of reality, such exploration involving a close scrutiny of linguistic features and a critical consideration of their possible literary effects. A poem is complete and self-contained and patterned, and so implies a stability and a coherence even when what is expressed seems to be fleeting and disparate. So it is in the Rosenberg poem, for example, or in the first of Sassoon's, two kinds of conflicting awareness come together in the mood and impression of a passing moment, and are held poised in the pattern of the poem. And in Sassoon's second poem, we have the sound of actual utterance, particular remarks set in direct speech. And yet, of course, they are at the same time not particular at all, any more than being scarlet, bald and short of breath, having a puffy and petulant face are general descriptive details of a plurality of majors. The difference between the particular and the general, which would usually need to be honoured in referential description, is here fused into a reality which is not referentially consistent or objectively true to life, but which is consistent with the representational patterning of sound in phrases like *puffy*, *petulant*, and *guzzling and gulping*, and is subjectively true to the mood of the moment.

I suggest, then, that two kinds of awareness might emerge from these activities. Firstly, there is the awareness that different formulations of propositional content express different realities; that even the slightest of changes has potential significance for interpretation. This is, in principle, true of all texts. But in poetry, I have argued, the detachment from outside context and the consequent self-contained patterning of language, implying as it does a deliberate fashioning of form, reduces the usual redundancies of language use, focuses attention on the text itself and presupposes that all elements in it interrelate as parts of the whole, and contribute to coherence. In this respect, poetry always has designs upon us; and it always challenges us to find the wavelength of its meanings by fine tuning.

The second kind of awareness is that these different realities that poetry represents are of their nature both fugitive and yet unchanging. They are bound to be fugitive because they are compounded of what can only be referentially expressed as distinct; they are a realignment of established ways of thought and expression and so obviously cannot be accountable to these established ways. So they are a counter-reality, endlessly elusive and constant only within the poem's context. But they are also changelessly preserved, held in the order established by the patterning of language which creates that context; and endlessly recurring at every reading.

Returning now to the present business of practical demonstration, I want to consider another example of the derivation of poems from a passage of authorized prose. In the case of the poems derived from the Sassoon passages, the object of the exercise was to keep as close to the original as possible, drawing on its phrases, and seeking to give representational force to its referential meaning. In this respect, the prose and poetry were consistent in style, and expressed the same first-person perspectives on the scene described. I want now to look at a very different kind of authorized text, and a very different kind of poetic derivation, to see how these might be turned to pedagogic advantage. In this case, the derived poem is already provided and so, in this sense, has its own authority.

The text is a letter written in the nineteenth century by a girl to her sweetheart. It originally appeared, with an accompanying poem, in a publication printed in 1871 and entitled, rather cumbrously (and obscurely):

> *The Curiosities of Street Literature Comprising Cocks or Catchpennies, a large and curious assortment of street drolleries, squibs, Histories, comic tales in verse and prose*

A Love Letter from Sarah to Charles

The following epistle was written by a girl at Deal to her sweetheart, a sailor on board a man of war in the Downs. The lieutenant of the ship found it on board, twisted up with tobacco in it, by which it seems our seafaring spark had as little regard for his mistress, after enjoyment, as if he had been of more illustrious rank.

Lovin Der Charls,
This mi kind love to yow is to tell yow, after all owr sport and fon, I am lik to pay fort, for I am with child; and wors of al, my sister Nan knos it, and cals me hore and bech, and is redy to ter my sol owt, and curs Jack Peny lies with her evry tim he cums ashor; and the saci dog wold have lade with me to, but I wold not let him, for I wil be always honest to yow; therfor der Charls come ashor, and let us be mared to safe my vartu: and if yow have no munni, I will paun my new stais and sel mi new smoks yow gave me, and that will pay the parsen and find us a diner; and pray der lovin Charls cum ashor, and der Charls dont be frad for wont of a ring, for I have stole mi sister Nans, and the nasty tod shall never have it no mor; for she tels abot that I am goin to have a bastard, and God bles yowr lovin sol cum sune, for I longs to be mared accordin to yowr promis, and I will be yowr der vartus wife til deth,
Sarah Johnson

PS.—Pray dont let yowr mesmat Jack se this, if yow do hel tel owr Nan, and shel ter mi hart owt then, for shes a devil at me now.

To this is appended 'a poetical version of the foregoing' as follows:

> Dear object of my love, whose manly charms
> With bliss extatic fill'd my circling arms;
> That bliss is past, and nought for me remains
> But dire reproach, and sharp unpitied pains:
> For (Death to me, and food to others pride)
> My sister has my growing shame descry'd,
> Ev'n she assails me with opprobrious name,
> When the prude's conscious she deserves the same:
> Her loose associate, sated, from her flies,
> And vainly to seduce my virtue tries:
> True, as a wife, I only want the name;
> O! haste and wed me, and preserve my fame.
> Unlike most modern matches ours shall be,
> From settlement, the lawyer's fetters, free;
> I'll quit my All, and be content with thee.
> Then haste away, and strike detraction dead;
> The nuptial feast awaits you, and the bed;
> Nor fear the hand that will endure for life,
> With me, your loving and your faithful wife.
>
> POSTSCRIPT
> These earnest dictates of my anxious heart
> I beg you will not to your friend impart;
> For oft beneath fair friendship's specious show,
> The traitor lurks, the undermining foe.
> R.A.[14]

A number of differences between Sarah's letter and the poetical version will be readily observed. Her idiosyncratic spelling has, to begin with, been restored to conventional form. But even if we were to rewrite her letter so that it conformed to standards of correctness (a task that students could, as an interesting language exercise, be asked to carry out), differences between the texts still very markedly remain. The style, we might say, is quite different: in the one text it is simple and direct, and in the other ornate and formal. What do these terms mean? Can we give these impressions a more precise description? We move in on the language. Consider the grammar. In the letter we have a simple linear sequence of co-ordinate clauses linked by simple conjunctions (*and, but, for*); the noun phrases are generally bare of any adornment. In the poetical version, the syntax is much more complex, with noun phrases in particular heavily loaded with elaboration. Even more striking, perhaps, are the lexical differences between the texts. Apart from the heavy-duty function items like *of, all, with, to,* and so on, which are bound to occur, ex officio, so to speak, the vocabulary of these two texts does not correspond at all: they hardly have a single full-blown lexical item in common. They express the same state of affairs in entirely different terms. But is it the same state of affairs? What is the effect of the verbal elaboration of the poetical version? We move from a consideration of the language to its literary significance. What does the poem represent?

To begin with, it clearly does not represent the personal experience of poor Sarah Johnson. It is not her point of view or her voice that we hear. Her *sport and fun* are transformed into *bliss extatic*; *whore and bitch* become *dire reproach* and *opprobrious name*. These expressions are not part of her vocabulary. They have, we might suggest, a self-conscious formality which puts us at a distance from the immediacy of the experience, makes it more general, depersonalizes it. All of the actual people disappear. Nan, that nasty toad, ready to tear Sarah's soul out, is abstracted into a tame prude and an unnamed sister. Charles, so often apostrophized in the letter in continuing and poignant appeal, has his name and identity replaced by *Dear object of my love*. He indeed becomes an object rather than a person: we are not even told that he is a sailor; he could be anybody. And his messmate, cursed Jack Penny, that saucy dog, is similarly depersonalized to become a *loose associate*. There is little hint of Sarah's distress, and no mention of her proposal to pawn her new stays and smocks, or of the stealing of her sister's ring.

What might be concluded from all this, then, is that the poetical version abstracts generalities out of the specific details of the original and expresses these in grammar and lexis whose very complexity and formality represent this abstraction, this distancing from immediate actuality. Although the poem is written in the first person, it at the same time adopts a third-person perspective in that it does not express the particulars of individual experience but extrapolates its more general features, thus allowing readers to recognize more readily its relevance to themselves. But if the poem generalizes in this way to the expression of common

experience, then it surely approximates to conventional statement, and loses its point as a poem. This raises again the question
of aesthetic quality discussed earlier in the book. We may call this
a poetical version because it is in verse, but does it have any of the
effects we would usually associate with poetry? I will take up this
matter in a moment.

But first we might present students with an alternative poetic
derivation, or one assembled with their participation, given the
kind of guidance I have suggested in previous activities. The aim
here would be (as with the poetic derivations from the Sassoon
passages) to make as much use of the original wording as possible,
and try to retain the individual features of the text. If students are
to participate in the composition of the derived poem, the first
step might be to work on regularizing the spelling of the letter, and
then, perhaps, to offer a first verse and indicate possible compo-
nents for the poem in the regularized text, to be ordered and
added to as required. As follows:

Loving dear Charles,
This, my kind love to you, *is to tell* you, after *all our sport and*
fun, I am like to pay for it, for I am with child; and *worst of all,*
my sister Nan knows it, and calls me whore and bitch, and is
ready to tear my soul out, and *cursed Jack Penny lies with her*
every time he comes ashore; and *the saucy dog would have laid*
with me too, but *I would not let him,* for I will be *always honest*
to you; therefore dear Charles come ashore, and *let us be mar-*
ried to save my virtue: and *if you have no money,* I will *pawn*
my new stays and *sell my new smocks you gave me,* and that
will *pay the parson* and find us a dinner; and pray dear loving
Charles come ashore, and dear Charles *don't be afraid for want*
of a ring, for I have stolen my sister Nan's, and the nasty toad
shall never have it no *more;* for she tells about that I am going
to have a bastard, and *God bless your loving soul come soon,*
for *I long to be married* according to your promise, and I will be
your dear *virtuous wife till death,*
    Sarah Johnson

Loving dear Charles, this is to tell
That I am like to pay
For all our sport and fun, for I
Am in the family way.

One might also provide a word or phrase or two which do not appear in the original text: *according to your vow, I long with every breath, fee,* and give any other guidance that seems appropriate.

We might proceed by first looking in the text for rhyming words and assembling the parts into metrical units. For example:

and cursed Jack Penny lies with her
and worst of all, my sister Nan

knows it and calls me *whore*
each time he comes *ashore*
shall never have it *more*

would have laid with me *too*
honest always to *you*

God bless your loving soul, come soon
Your virtuous wife till death

The derived poem could come out looking like this:

Loving dear Charles, this is to tell
That I am like to pay
For all our sport and fun, for I
Am in the family way.

And worst of all, my sister Nan
Knows it and calls me whore.
And cursed Jack Penny lies with her
Each time he comes ashore.

The saucy dog Jack Penny, he
Would have laid with me too.
I would not let him, loving Charles,
Honest always to you.

Therefore, come ashore, dear Charles,
Let us be married now,
To save my virtue, loving Charles,
According to your vow.

And if you have no money, Charles,
My new smocks you gave me
I'll sell, and pawn my stays as well,
To pay the parson's fee.

Do not, for want of a ring, dear Charles,
Be afraid to come ashore,
For I have stolen my sister Nan's:
She shall never have it more.

God bless your loving soul, come soon,
For I long with every breath
To be married, Charles, so I can be
Your virtuous wife till death.

A comparison between this and the previous derivation can set the scene for further developments along two lines. First there is the question raised earlier about aesthetic quality. The first version seemed to be little more than the ornate assertion of conventional values. This second one, in contrast, seems to be little more than a shuffling of prosaic phrases. Both seem banal: the first because it is too general and the second because it is too particular. Is there any significance to be found in either? What, if anything, is the poetic point? One way of considering these questions would be to set these versions alongside authorized poems on a similar theme. The essential thing to note is that it is precisely the purpose of these derivations and intertextual comparisons to stimulate thinking on questions such as these about the nature of poetic meaning. If these versions seem to lack some essential feature of poetic representation, what is it? And can they be modified to provide for the inadequacy? The work outlined in this chapter is intended to bring these issues (discussed in Chapter 9 in the first part of the book) within the scope of practical classroom enquiry.

A second line of development leads into a consideration not so much of the essential significance of poetry in general, but of the differences between more particular poetic styles and genres. The first of our versions is elaborately wrought within its rhyming couplets, an instance of stylized eloquence, self-consciously formal. The second is a ballad, a popular form of verse which is closer to oral narrative tradition and has no such pretension to social status in the polite world. What kinds of topic, perspective, point of view, voice are these different genres most appropriately designed to represent? The comparison of our versions, both derived from the same textual source, should be an effective way of initiating discussion on the question. I shall return to this matter of difference of poetic idiom in a subsequent chapter.

Meanwhile, there is one further point that might be made in this chapter: one which I mentioned at the very beginning of the book. It is that although, as I have argued, poetry needs to be taken seriously, this does not mean that it must always be serious. Poor Sarah Johnson is a sad figure, but her situation has always been the subject of vulgar ribaldry in a male-dominated world. Alongside the versions we have already considered, therefore, we can set an irreverent one along the following lines:

> Charles, an amorous seafarer
> Went ashore and boarded Sarah.
> Now Sarah wants to go to church,
> But Charles has left her in the lurch.
> He's back on board his ship, for he
> Is just not mariner you see.

It might be objected that this is a typical piece of deplorable male sexism. And so it is. It represents reality from a particular perspective. But the mistake is to suppose that this can be absolute or have any special authority. It is this mistake which, as I have argued, it is one of the educational purposes of poetry to expose. And that is the point of giving a place to poetry of an irreverent and ribald kind. This too is a matter I shall be returning to later.

10 Progressive derivation: composing interim versions

In the preceding chapters we have been looking at activities whereby passages of authorized prose serve as reference for the comparison of poetic texts, both of a derived and authorized kind. I want now to propose a variant on this procedure. Our starting point in this case is an authorized poem. We rewrite it in prose and then produce for critical consideration a sequence of reformulations which gradually approximate to the original text. The writing of the prose version and the transitional variants will be based, of course, on a reading of the original which identifies certain of its features as of particular significance. The idea, obviously enough, is to show a poem taking shape and so to direct attention to these features of the original as they emerge through the interim stages. The purpose is still to compare, but the comparison now is not between poems (derived or authorized) in a completed state, but between different phases in a composing process. An example:

Text A

There were a number of white chickens in the farmyard and an old wheelbarrow shining in the rain.

Text B

A red wheelbarrow
shines in the rain
beside white chickens.

How is Text B different from Text A? To begin with the obvious, the text is differently arranged on the page; instead of being horizontally connected, as in the prose, it is vertically assembled, one phrase above the other. It takes on the appearance of poetry. So what is the effect of this? Well, it might be suggested, we tend to read it differently. We assume Text A to be an extract from some longer description, a fragment, a part which patterns in with some other pieces of text which are missing. The very use of the definite article implies this: *the* farmyard. Which one is being referred to, and what is the point of referring to it anyway? We assume that we can only know this by restoring the extract to its proper place in context. What then of Text B? Well, it looks less like a fragment; it does not seem to depend on being connected up with a missing text. Why not? It has something to do, perhaps, with the way the language is arranged. When language is arranged in the normal way, as in prose, in a horizontal line, then you naturally look for connections at each end. But the vertical arrangement, as in Text B, has already cut connections of this kind by separating the parts of the sentence and putting them in parallel. This alone seems to suggest that they have already been disconnected from any other text, and make up a text of their own. They have been assembled into a pattern already, and so they have no need to be patterned into anything else. So they can be read as having a meaning in their own right, enclosed within the text. What, then, might this meaning be? Well, since we cannot look elsewhere, let us see whether a closer look at the language might give us some indication. How, then, is the language of Text B different from that of the prose passage?

The farmyard with its definite reference is gone. The tense has shifted from past to present, and the participle has been converted into a finite verb (*shining—shines*). So what? The observations are, we might suggest, now located in the here and now by the use of the simple present, and the shining is no longer an incidental quality of the wheelbarrow expressed as a dependent phrase, but an action, expressed as a main verb, something the wheelbarrow does. *The* wheelbarrow? The text has *a* wheelbarrow. Does this mean a particular actual wheelbarrow (one I am looking at now) or a general and abstract wheelbarrow (any old wheelbarrow)? Well, Text B (as distinct from Text A) could be read either way. A particular wheelbarrow, here in front of my very eyes, and, as it happens, among white chickens, shines in the rain. Or a wheelbarrow—wheelbarrows in general—will shine in the rain when they are among white chickens. In the first case, the white chickens are incidental, but in the second they are conditional. Text B, we might suggest, lends itself to both a particular and a general reading; there is a congruence of different perspectives. But notice that it is not just a wheelbarrow but a *red* wheelbarrow. The change of adjective (from *old* to *red*) sets up a contrast with the *white* chickens. And this, perhaps, draws our attention to two further contrasts between the nouns themselves: a singular and inanimate wheelbarrow is among the plural and animate chickens. What significance might there be in such oppositions, especially when set alongside the fusion of particular and general that we noticed earlier? The lines somehow seem to be expressing contrast and congruence at the same time.

And so we encourage the close scrutiny of the text, analysing the language and speculating on its possible significance. Then, at what seems to be a propitious moment, we can introduce two further interim texts. For example:

Text C

A red wheelbarrow
glazed with rain
beside the white chickens.

Text D

A red wheel
barrow
glazed with rain
water
beside the white
chickens.

What differences do we notice between Text B and Text C? Most obviously, the second line has changed. The finite verb *shines* has disappeared, to be replaced by the past participle of a different verb altogether: *glazed*. The description now no longer takes the form of a sentence but of a noun phrase, and so is even more detached from any location in time. And the wheelbarrow no longer actively shines *in the rain* but is in a state of being—glazed *with rain*. There is an additional point of contrast between the noun phrases in the first and third lines: *a* red wheelbarrow, but *the* white chickens. What, then, might be read into these changes? Do the lines express a perception of contrasts held stable in detachment from place, in a moment out of time? And what of Text D?

The only addition here is the single word *water*. But the text has changed its shape on the page. It has taken on a more distinctive pattern. It is now a poem of six lines, and lines 2, 4, and 6 each consist of a single word of two syllables. Such patterning might be said to give form to the momentary stability mentioned earlier. But then the words of lines 2 and 4 also seem to have an opposite destabilizing effect in that they take us somewhat by surprise. The preceding lines are complete noun phrases in themselves and we take them in as such. Thus, in line 1 we read *a red wheel* as a completed unit of meaning. But then *barrow* appears and we have to make an adjustment to accommodate it. And the same thing happens in the next line: *glazed with rain* is a completed unit, but again we have to readjust as *water* appears in the next line. What are we to make of this? The normal perception of ordinary and unitary things like a wheelbarrow or rainwater is disrupted (it might be suggested) and realigned into an alternative pattern, and within this pattern, contrasts coexist and are made coherent, if only for a moment. Thus the particular can be represented as having a more general significance while retaining its particularity. So much in poetry, we might say, depends upon such a recognition. At this point we can present the authorized poem.

The Red Wheelbarrow

so much depends
upon

a red wheel
barrow

glazed with rain
water

beside the white
chickens.
(William Carlos Williams)

The progression through these different stages of composition has, we could argue, indeed demonstrated how much depends on such apparently simple and inconsequential perceptions, but only when represented in this way and enclosed within the patterns of the poem.

Having sharpened student perception of the significance of

linguistic features by comparing interim reformulations in this way, we might then, following previous procedure, invite them to compare the authorized poem by Williams with a derived one which verbalizes some part of the proposed interpretation more explicitly. The following, for example, could be used for this purpose.

A Moment's Image

The farm is here. The farmyard now,
    after the rain.
Here and now. A moment's image I
    try to retain.

Here and now. Red wheelbarrow,
    bright in the wet,
beside white chickens. Farmyard.
    The moment goes. Yet

So much depends on this. The image
    the words contain:
White chickens, red wheelbarrow
    glazed with rain.[15]

The comparison between the authorized and derived poems could well, of course, activate interpretations of the original which have not been presupposed in the interim versions. This is all to the good, for the purpose of these versions is not to restrict students to one convergent and definitive meaning. This is not the end in view: quite the contrary. Indeed, the focus of attention in this activity is meant to be not on the end but the means, the interpretative process and not its conclusion. The idea is to sharpen students' perception of linguistic features and make them aware of their possible significance so that this perception and this awareness can be exercised in the achievement of their own meanings, both in respect to this poem and to others. I have referred to original poems as authorized. The term 'authentic' could be used as a synonym. But although an authorized text and an authentic text can be seen as the same thing, an authorized interpretation is entirely different from an authentic one. They are, indeed, contradictory. According to the arguments I have been pursuing in this book, to accept an authorized interpretation of a poem is to deny the possibility of an authentic reaction to it—a reaction which it is of the very nature of poetry to provoke. In general terms, the whole purpose of the activities I am proposing here is to develop in students the ability to authenticate poetic texts as poems on their own authority.

11   Using prose paraphrases

I want now to consider activities which, like those just outlined, take an authorized poem as their starting point, but which then develop rather differently. In this case, instead of beginning with a prose version which alters the words of the original, and then gradually reinstates them in successive variants, we produce a paraphrase version which incorporates the original text and expands upon it by additional description and comment. We then present two poetic texts, one of which is the authorized original and the other a derivation, and ask students to make comparisons between the two as representations of the prose version, evaluate their relative aesthetic value, and, in the light of this, say which they think is the genuine article and which the fake. It is important that the original should not be identified in advance, since this would almost certainly dispose them to give it preferential treatment. Here is an example. All I will say at this point (so as to allow readers to exercise their own critical faculties) is that the original is a poem by A.E. Housman entitled:

Eight o'Clock

Text A

The prisoner was brought out on to the scaffold just before eight o'clock in the morning. Below him a crowd of people had gathered in the market-place to watch his execution. He stood there, his arms strapped to his sides. The noose was put around his neck. There was a rumble of muttering from the watching crowd. Then the clock in the church steeple on the other side of the square began to chime out the quarters of the hour: one, two, three, four ... In the brief silence before the first stroke of eight, the crowd became quite still. Then, at the first stroke of the hour, there was a sudden movement: the man dropped and was jerked abruptly to a stop, his body twitching on the end of the rope. The clock went on with its chiming. The people started slowly to disperse, and to go about their business.

Text B

The clock in the church steeple
    Sounded the quarters for the hour of eight.
In the market-place he saw the crowd of people
    Awaiting his fate.

Strapped and noosed, head bowed,
    He stood and heard the clock chime in the tower.
Then in the sudden silence of the crowd
    It struck the hour.

Text C

He stood, and heard the steeple
    Sprinkle the quarters on the morning town.
One, two, three, four, to market-place and people
    It tossed them down.

Strapped, noosed, nighing his hour,
    He stood and counted them and cursed his luck;
And then the clock collected in the tower
    Its strength, and struck.

There are a number of points that might emerge from discussion. In the prose text, for example, the scene is described in detachment. *He* takes on its normal third-person value in that what is said about the condemned man is observable in the usual referential way. The reader is cast in the role of bystander, a witness to the event: there he was, his arms strapped, neck in a noose, head bowed. In the poetic texts the perspective is different, and the third-person pronoun takes on something of first-person value. We are told things which cannot be observed but only experienced, a matter of *first*-person perception. So in Text B it is not simply that there was a crowd of people, but he *saw* them; in both poetic texts, he *heard* the sounds of the clock, and in Text C he counted its chimes and cursed his luck (presumably in his head). These referential impossibilities indicate that, though the third-person pronoun is being used, it is not just a third-person *he* which is being referred to, but the experience of a first-person *I* which is being represented.

What, then, we might go on to ask, of the other things involved in the event. What, for example, of the *it* of the third-person clock? In Text B the clock seems to behave in a fairly straight-forward way: it sounds out the quarters, it chimes, it strikes, all in proper referential fashion. But in Text C it does things we would normally associate not with an inanimate object but with an animate, indeed human, being. *It* takes on the life of *he* or *she*. It sprinkles the quarters of the hour, it tosses them down on the people below (*sprinkles, quarters, tosses down*: what do these words suggest?). It collects its strength before it strikes. And now notice how this last action is described. The noun phrase *its strength* is displaced from its normal syntactic position, held back by the intervening adverbial phrase, and prosodically by the pause at the end of the line. And this disrupted grammar is in contrast with the simple sequence of co-ordinate clauses in the line before. What is the effect of this? Well, the impression of slow motion, perhaps, with time held back with the arrested movement of the syntax. This is no detached description of an event. It is the ex-pression of how it might be experienced. The language represents the clock's slow gathering together of its strength, the moment of suspense and suspended time, and the final blow in the last alliter-ative and monosyllabic verb which ends the poem, and ends the life of the condemned man at the same time.

Are similar effects achieved in Text B? Here, too, there is a dis-ruption of normal syntactic sequence in the last two lines which we might say suggests the arrest of time. The striking of the hour is held back. But in this case the adverbial intervention has to do not with the clock but the crowd. The pause before the striking of the hour is charged not with suspense but with silence. There is in this poem no animation in the clock. When it strikes, it simply strikes the hour: there is no suggestion of a human blow. Indeed, one obvious difference between the two poems is that in Text B it is the crowd which is given prominence, whereas in Text C it is the clock.

In this way, then, students can be encouraged and guided into an investigation of possible significance by intertextual compari-son. Which features of the prose description does each poem focus on and how are these represented? Could other poetic versions be derived from it which emphasized other features: the contrast, for example, between the individual and the crowd, the end of his life and the continuation of theirs, both marked by the measurement of time sounded out from the church steeple? Could these poems be changed so as to alter their focus and their effect? How would you compare them in respect to their aesthetic value? Which do you prefer and why? And which do you think is the fake? There is no reason, of course, why we should not derive, or get students to derive, more than one poetic text from the prose paraphrase, and so provide more data for critical comparison. Here, for example, is another effort, in a different style, that could be set alongside those we have been considering:

Text D

He sees the crowd of people there,
Watching in the market-square.

The noose is round his neck. They wait.
The church clock strikes the hour of eight.

His time has come. He has to die.
The crowd disperses. Time goes by.

Not much of a masterpiece, you might say. But that does not matter, so long as it provokes an enquiry into the different ways in which language can be used to poetic effect.

That perhaps is enough by way of demonstration of this particular activity. Should readers be interested in doing comparative critical analysis for themselves on sets of texts, along the lines I have suggested (or along any other lines, if it comes to that), I have provided further examples in the Appendix. But I want now to move on to a variant of the procedures I have been proposing in this chapter.

12 Comparing derived and authorized versions

As an alternative to the procedures just demonstrated, or as a development from them, we could dispense with the prose derivation and simply present poetic texts for comparison. In this case we would derive versions with different degrees of modification directly from the authorized poem. As before, students would then be asked to consider the differences and suggest what significance they might have. Here, for example, is a set of such texts: an authorized poem by Robert Frost together with two unauthorized versions.

Fireflies in the Garden

Text A

Here come real stars. They fill the upper skies.
And here on earth come emulating flies.
Though they were never really stars at heart,
These flies achieve at times a star-like start.

Text B

Here on earth come little star-like flies
To emulate real stars in upper skies.
Although flies cannot equal stars in size,
(And flies were never really stars at heart)
These flies achieve at times a star-like start.
Only of course they can't sustain the part.

Text C

Here come real stars to fill the upper skies,
And here on earth come emulating flies,
That though they never equal stars in size,

(And they were never really stars at heart)
Achieve at times a very star-like start.
Only, of course, they can't sustain the part.

What differences might be noted here, and what points about their effect might be made in discussion? Perhaps (among others) the following. Text A looks very like a derivation. It is basically Text C with two lines left out and some minor adjustments made to the syntax. As a result, there is a shift in focus of content: the poem is about what the fireflies achieve rather than on their limitations and it ends on a note of success rather than failure. But what of the syntax? To begin with, this text consists of four separate sentences, whereas the corresponding lines in Text C consist of only one. The first line is divided into two sentences rather than one by replacing the conjunction *to* with the pronoun *they*. Let us pause a moment at this pronoun. Does it appear in Text C? Yes, it does: three times. What does it refer to? The fireflies. Does it ever refer to the stars? No. Whenever the stars are mentioned they are given full lexical reference.

What about Text B? This corresponds quite closely to Text C: it is essentially composed of the same lines, but these have been shuffled about a bit. The first two lines are reversed, so we start with the fireflies and not the stars, and they constitute a separate sentence. The status (so to speak) of these flies and the contrast with the stars they emulate is more explicitly spelled out by the adjectives *little* (which anticipates line 3) and *star-like* (which anticipates line 2). What about the pronoun *they* that we were talking about before? It only occurs once, in the last line (in reference to the flies). Up to that point, all references are fully lexical.

What, then, can we make of all this? What possible significance, for example, can we attach to all this rather pernickety business of pronouns and reference? Well, consider the function of pronouns in general. What do they do? They are *pro*–nouns, they stand in for them, substitute for them, take on something of their identity. And this, of course, is just what the fireflies do in these texts: they are star-like, pro-stellar objects, but no more equal to stars in size than pronouns are equal to full lexical reference. In both cases, we have reduced, temporary substitutes for the real thing. So it is entirely appropriate, we might conclude, that reference to the fireflies should be by pronoun, whereas reference to the stars, the real thing, should be fully lexical. In this way, we might say, their shortlived emulation is indeed not a matter of reference, but of representation. But in Text B, the flies are given equal lexical status with what they are emulating. One might say, indeed, that their separate identity seems to be emphasized. In lines 3 and 4, for example, the repeated lexical items seem to be obtrusive: it would be more natural to pronominalize:

Although *they* cannot equal stars in size,
(And *they* were never really stars at heart)

But this emphasized lexical status is, of course, consistent with the fact that this text begins with the flies, and establishes them as the topic in their own independent clause. The stars, on the other hand, appear in a dependent clause, relegated to a secondary position. The emulation takes precedence over what is real. In Text C the opposite happens: the real stars come first, and in subsequent appearances they are never reduced in lexical status. With the flies, on the other hand, once having made a lexical appearance, and in that respect making a star-like start, all they can manage afterwards is a pronominal presence. They cannot sustain the part. We might suggest, in view of this, that Text C represents the theme of emulation and its failure in a way that Text B does not.

On the other hand, there is also something to be said for Text B. The recurrent lexical reference, and the avoidance of pronouns, may be said to represent a stubborn assertion of separate identity, so that the eventual appearance of the pronoun in the last line expresses its failure, and a submission to reduced and dependent status, with particular force. We could argue that this poem, therefore, represents the striving to sustain equality in a way that of Text C does not, since in that poem the failure of such effort is presupposed in the use of language from the very beginning. But then if the last line of Text B is to carry such significance we might have expected it to have the kind of prominence it has in Text C, where it stands out as a single sentence enclosed within a metrical line after the previous complex sentence has extended over all of the preceding five lines. In Text B the last line does not have quite the same punch-line effect.

A final observation might be made about lexical meanings. In all of the texts there is the play on words between *star* and *start*: the second word does indeed quite literally (phonologically/graphologically) have a star-like start in its sound and spelling. There is also a possible play on two meanings of the word *star* itself. In one sense, the word means a heavenly body, but in another, of course, it means a celebrity, especially from the world of entertainment. This second sense is perhaps particularly activated by the word *part*, and suggests another meaning that might be read into Texts B and C, namely that these fireflies have their human counterparts who make similar attempts at emulation, but which cannot be long sustained.

And so we explore possibilities of meaning in these three texts, not, to repeat the point already made, to home in on a particular interpretation, but to activate the process of interpreting by exploring the implications of different uses of language.

As I indicated earlier, the derivations that are provided for comparison are designed so as to draw attention to features of the original (which is Text C, by the way, of those we have just been considering) which seem to be, on one interpretation at least, of particular significance. These derived versions might depart from the authorized poem in only one or two particulars, or they might differ in more radical ways. I want now to consider texts which give some idea of this derivational range and suggest how it might be put to pedagogic use. We continue the topic of insect life but move from fireflies to butterflies. The original is a poem by Robert Graves.[16] Here it is in the company of a derived version in which the modifications are, though significant, on a relatively small scale.

Flying Crooked

Text A

The butterfly, a cabbage-white,
(His honest idiocy of flight)
Will never now, it is too late,
Master the art of flying straight,
Yet has—who knows so well as I?—
A just sense of how not to fly:
He lurches here and here by guess
And God and hope and hopelessness.
Even the aerobatic swift
Has not his flying-crooked gift.

Text B

This butterfly, a cabbage-white,
Follows a most erratic flight.
It is too late to learn instead
The art of flying straight ahead.
And yet it has, as well as I,
A just sense of how not to fly.
It lurches here and there by guess,
And God and hope and hopelessness.
Even the aerobatic swift
Has not this flying-crooked gift.

What differences are to be noted here? To begin with, the syntax in Text B is more regular in arrangement. Each pair of rhyming couplets neatly encloses a complete sentence. The poem is well ordered. In Text A, on the other hand, there is no such neatness of pattern. It begins, as does Text B, with two noun phrases in apposition. Since we assume these to be the subject, we anticipate the appearance of a finite verb to continue the structure in the normal way. In Text B we get one: *follows*. But in Text A we don't. Instead we get an aside in parentheses which postpones the appearance. Then, at the beginning of the next line, the continuity of the structure is resumed with the finite verb *will*. But this is an auxiliary, of course, and as such it sets up the expectation that a lexical verb will follow to complete the phrase. The expectation is so strong that I have found that when you ask people who do not know the text to read it aloud for the first time, without preparation, they will tend to read *will never now* as *will never know* (influenced also, perhaps, by the formulaic familiarity of this verbal pattern, and a peripheral perception of the word *know* two lines later). The completion is further arrested by the intrusion of another parenthetical element, this time between commas. Then, at last, the lexical verb appears and is followed by an object noun phrase: *master the art of flying straight*; the syntax is finally complete. And yet, no. Just as we thought we had done with this structure and arrived at a closure, it continues into the next line: *Yet has* ... Yet has what? Again our expectation is deferred with another parenthetical comment, this time between dashes. There is no regularity even in the way the disruptions are indicated: parentheses, commas, dashes.

In short, in comparison with the ordered and predictable

sequences of Text B, the grammar of Text A is all over the place. But then that, of course, is in a way just as it should be, for the butterfly is all over the place as well. Its crooked flight is represented by the crooked disposition of the language. The grammar sets us off in one direction, and then unexpectedly changes course. It lurches. And in Text A it does not even lurch here and there, which would conform to some expected pattern of phrase, but here and *here*. In short, this text can be said to represent what the poem is about in a way in which Text B does not. How is this conclusion supported by other differences between the two texts: *the* butterfly in Text A, *this* butterfly in Text B, and the difference of phrasing in the last line? How indeed?

And what, after all, *is* the poem about? The crooked flight of the cabbage-white butterfly? Why should this be thought to be worthy of notice? The fifth line of each text provides perhaps something of a clue. The first person here seems to identify with the butterfly in not flying straight, in having a sense of how not to fly. How might we interpret this? Perhaps it suggests that poetry is also the expression of this sense, the avoidance, clearly in evidence in the grammar of Text A, of what is straightforward and direct and in conformity with expectation. The poet, we might say, has the gift of writing crooked. But, of course, this crookedness is neverthless captured in patterned language, so that although there is no straightforward direction, the flight and the writing are far from aimless. The word *lurches* suggests a sort of clumsy randomness of movement, which, we might suggest, is particularly well represented by Text A. But that representation is itself not clumsy or random. It is carefully crafted in the shape of the language.

So far we have been comparing two poetic texts which, though different in detail, and significantly so, do nevertheless have many features in common, and are, in content and in style, recognizably versions of the 'same' poem, variable clones, so to speak. We might now present, for further comparison, two other poems which are much further along the derivational range in that they incorporate changes of a much more radical kind.

Text C

I watched a butterfly, a cabbage white,
Lurching across a field in crooked flight.
I watched it pass and thought: it is too late

For it to learn the art of flying straight,
The deft direction-finding of the swift.
Yet flying crooked also is a gift.

Text D

                  does not fly
The butterfly   straight;

It finds   by hope and
        its way   fate.
                        gift
But flying   a
            crooked is

Denied the aerobatic swift.

I recognize   mine,
            this gift as

        predictably
Un   off-
                      line.

How do these two poems differ from the others? Take Texts A
and C, for instance. We might begin by drawing attention to the
grammar of the opening lines in each case. In Text A, the subject
of the sentence is the butterfly; and it is, we might say, put up front
as the topic. In Text C, on the other hand, the butterfly is the
object: the subject of the sentence is the first-person pronoun *I*.
One might infer from this that whereas the first of these poems is
about the butterfly, the second is about the person observing it,
and this inference is given further support by the fact that in Text
C there is a parallel recurrence of the opening noun phrase *I*
watched in line 3, and by the fact that the only time the first person
occurs in Text A is in a comment in passing, an aside between
dashes (—*who knows so well as I?*—), which is therefore not
really part of the grammatical structure of the poem at all. It might
be suggested too that the status of the butterfly as topic in Text A
is enhanced by its being humanized: the pronoun used is *he* and
not, as in Text C (and all the other texts), *it*. The only human presence in these other poems is the first person, and this presence is,
as I have already suggested, particularly prominent in Text C. We
might also notice that whereas the tense of Text A is in the present,
that of Text C is in the past.

What, then, might the significance be of these different linguistic features? The poem of Text A can be said to represent the actuality of the butterfly and its flight more directly, whereas the poem of Text C is a more detached description: here observation of the actual butterfly counts less, it would seem, than the observations that it gives rise to. The patterning of language does not, as it does in Text A, represent the butterfly by a kind of verbal mimicry. Instead, it seems to represent the process of reflection about an event in the past and at a remove from immediate perception (*I watched . . . and thought . . .*). The event is described and reflected upon in two complex sentences, the first extending over the first two lines, the second over the following three. Then comes a contrastive statement (*Yet . . .*) which, as a simple sentence contained within a single line, also contrasts in form with what has preceded. The contrast, then, is both stated and represented. The effect is to give weight to this last line and to give it the force of an apophthegm, a wise saying of some sort. In consequence (in conclusion indeed) the implication is stronger in this poem than in that of Text A that the crooked flying of the butterfly has some covert symbolic significance. The poem, we might suggest, is not primarily about a butterfly at all.

What, then, of Text D? Here the flight of the butterfly is represented by the actual disposition of words on the page: the lines themselves are crooked. At the same time, the significance of its flight is spelled out. The first four lines about the butterfly are given explicit point in the last two about the first-person poet. Both have the same gift. Both are unpredictably off-line. It might be said that the obviousness of the representation is matched by the explicitness of its significance. That might lead to the evaluative judgement that the poem lacks subtlety by its very neatness. On the other hand, of course, it might not. Students could make different observations and come to different conclusions, and they should feel free to do so. What I have done here is to suggest possibilities. As always, the purpose of comparison is not to converge on a single interpretation but to stimulate the process of enquiry into meaning.

The derived texts we have just been analysing are different kinds of poem from that of Texts A and B. Discussion of them, therefore, could develop into a closer examination of differences of style. This would lead us into more advanced exercises in literary critical awareness.

One line of enquiry might lead from Text D. Here the very substance of the language is fashioned into mimetic shape. We have come across this kind of thing before, but previously it was in respect to phonological patterning. In Part One, for example, we looked at the way attitudes (gaiety, boredom) were represented in a poem by Pope by alliteration and assonance, the recurrence of particular segments of sound. What we have in Text D is the same expressive principle applied to the visual medium of print: it is a kind of graphological alliteration. This visual mode of verbal art has a long history. The Greeks practised it in classical times. So did the English poet George Herbert in the seventeenth century, the French poet Guillaume Apollinaire in the nineteenth. In Chinese and Japanese poems, the written characters themselves are essential elements in the verbal design and they appeal to the eye as well as to the ear. This, of course, sets limits on their translation (of which more in a later chapter). Some modern European poets have focused on visual appeal as the main principle of composition. The result is what has been called concrete poetry. Here is an example:

(Alan Riddell: *Revolver*)

What, we might ask our students, are we to make of this? The word, so repeated, reversed, and arranged in a ring of letters challenges the reader to see significance in it which it would not have, either as a separate item of vocabulary, or as conventionally occurring in some context or other. The word is decomposed into its constituents and then recomposed into an alternative pattern. What does this pattern reveal? It might be noted that other words are contained within the circle: *love*, for example, and *evolve*. Following up this observation, it might be suggested that what is represented here is some sense of the endless continuity of love and evolution, some mystical assertion of the elemental life cycle, in contrast with what we would normally associate with the word *revolver* as a firearm, an instrument of death and destruction.

This, you may say, is somewhat fanciful. And so it is. But it is the effect of poetry (as I keep on insisting) to stimulate such flights of fancy. But the main point here is that this visual arrangement of even a single word can draw the attention of students to what I have called *poetentiality*—the way in which the latent possibilities for meaning in language can be exploited to poetic effect, alienating the reader from what is familiar so as to realign reality into a different order.

We might then go on to look at other examples of concrete poetry, or at instances in more traditional writing where the manipulation of the substantial features of language, aural and visual, seem to have particular significance. What, for example, does a particular rhyme scheme or metrical arrangement contribute to the meaning of a poem? What is the effect of transposing free verse into more regular prosodic form, and the reverse? A number of the derived versions that we have been comparing with the authorized originals have made prosodic changes. How do these changes impinge on interpretation? We might look at the graphological peculiarities of particular poets. Here is a verse from a poem by Emily Dickinson, for example:

My Life had stood — a Loaded Gun —
In Corners — till a Day
The Owner passed — identified —
And carried Me away —

Some words are made distinctive by the use of capital letters, and there is no conventional punctuation: dashes are used instead. Why? To what effect? e e cummings (*sic*) is also eccentric in his use of such graphological features (see his poem in the Appendix). Are the two poets eccentric in the same sort of way? We move here towards the more particular study of individual style.

And such study can also develop out of Text C, the third of the butterfly poems above. Consider its composition. It has six lines; the last of them is contrastive and set aside from the others in that it consists of a single and self-contained sentence; this last line expresses a final wise-sounding remark suggestive of some further symbolic significance in what is described. Where else have we encountered a poem like this? What does it call to mind? Consider the following:

Text C (Flying Crooked)

I watched a butterfly, a cabbage white,
Lurching across a field in crooked flight.
I watched it pass and thought: it is too late
For it to learn the art of flying straight,
The deft direction-finding of the swift.
Yet flying crooked also is a gift.

Fireflies in the Garden

Here come real stars to fill the upper skies,
And here on earth come emulating flies,
That though they never equal stars in size,
(And they were never really stars at heart)
Achieve at times a very star-like start.
Only, of course, they can't sustain the part.

The second of these poems is an authorized one by Robert Frost.
The first is pastiche, a version derived from an original poem by
Robert Graves (Text A, as a matter of fact), rewritten after the
manner of Frost. What is it, then, that characterizes this manner?
The comparisons we have already made will provide a starting
point for discussion and we could go on to look at other poems by
Frost, gradually in this way developing an awareness of his individual style. Thus we move from an understanding of poetry in
general towards an appreciation of the work of particular poets.
And this awareness might be further enhanced by the students'
own composition of pastiche or parody, and subsequently
extended beyond individual poets to take in different genres and
modes of poetic writing. I mentioned this as a possible line of
development at the end of Chapter 9 in reference to the different
versions of Sarah Johnson's sad letter to her lover. In the next
chapter I shall pursue this possibility a little further.

13   Comparing different modes of poetic writing

Let us then continue with Robert Frost and see how we might develop an awareness of his particular manner of writing, and subsequently how we might relate this to more general questions of poetic mode. Here is one of his best-known poems.[17]

Dust of Snow

The way a crow
Shook down on me
The dust of snow
From a hemlock tree

Has given my heart
A change of mood
And saved some part
Of a day I had rued.

As with the other Frost and Frost-like poems, we have the observation of a natural phenomenon (firefly, butterfly, crow) giving rise to reflection which hints at something significant beyond appearances: a theme behind the topic. The effect is to get the reader to ponder on what that might be. We can now set this poem alongside another which is topically similar. Conveniently, there is one which will serve our purpose by Theodore Roethke, another American poet and a contemporary of Frost (they both died in 1963, as it happens).

Night Crow

When I saw that clumsy crow
Flap from a wasted tree,
A shape in the mind rose up:
Over the gulfs of dream

Flew a tremendous bird
Further and further away
Into a moonless black,
Deep in the brain, far back.

What is the significance of the crow in each case? With Frost it
creates a mood in the heart, with Roethke a shape in the mind. In
Frost's poem it is associated with a hemlock tree and dust of snow,
in Roethke's with a wasted tree and the night, a moonless black.
And so comparisons can be made in the (by now) familiar way.
And these can be sharpened (again following procedures already
demonstrated) by reference to derived versions. Thus we might set
the following alongside the originals:

Text A (Dust of Snow)

When perching on a hemlock tree,
A crow shook down some snow on me.
This brought about a change of mood,
And saved part of a day I'd rued.

Text B (Night Crow)

When I saw that clumsy crow
Flap from a wasted tree,
Something inside my mind took shape,
A vision came to me:

Over the gulfs of dream there flew
Into a moonless black
A vast bird, further and further away,
Deep in the brain, far back.

The next stage is to consider to what extent, and with what consequences, one can recast one original poem in the form of the other.
Since our interest at the moment is in what is distinctive about
Frost's poetry, our task is to reformulate the Roethke poem. Here
is one attempt:

Text C (Night Crow)

When that crow
Flapped from a tree,
A shape in the mind
Rose up in me:

A tremendous bird,
So it would seem,
Flew further over
The gulfs of dream,

Further away
Into moonless black,
Deep in the brain,
Far back, far back.

Well, we might say, although the lines have been shortened and
rhymes introduced, so that the Roethke poem now has something
of the prosodic shape of Frost's, it does not read much like it
otherwise. Why not? For one thing, this has three verses rather
than two. Very well, let us try to derive another and more reduced
version, and at the same time try to capture a little of Frost's original phrasing. We might imagine something emerging along the
following lines:

Text D (Night Crow)

The way a crow
Flapped from a tree
Brought a shape to mind
And made me see

Over gulfs of dream
The bird fly back
Deep in the mind
Of moonless black.

We have now moulded Roethke's poem into something of a Frost-
like shape: thus, like the original, it consists of a single unpunctuated sentence contained within two simple verses which rhyme
on the second and fourth lines. We have lost a lot of Roethke in
the process of course. His poem has been stripped of almost all its
adjectives, for example: the crow is no longer clumsy, the tree no
longer wasted, and the tremendous bird has disappeared completely. But are we any closer to the Frost manner? Since this
manner is not tied uniquely to the particular form of this poem,
perhaps we can take another bearing on the question by trying to
fit Roethke into the shape of the Fireflies poem instead. We might

come up with something along the following lines:

Text E (Night Crow)

I saw a crow flap from a wasted tree
In clumsy movements as it seemed to me,
And in my mind it took shape as it flew
Of a vast bird of darkness that I knew.
Over the gulfs of dream it flies far back
Deep into the mind and moonless black.

This time we have managed to retain most of the content of the Roethke poem. But have we changed its meaning, and if so how? And have we caught something of the Frost effect?

So far we have been looking at ways in which a critical awareness of the characteristic features of Frost's poetry might be developed by getting students to compare reformulations of another author's poem and, as the awareness grows, to compose variants for themselves. We are using the same principles of composition and comparison of texts which have been demonstrated earlier, but now directed towards a greater sensitivity to individual style, to what is specific about a particular poet's way of writing. But we can follow the same principles in studying more general differences in poetic idiom or genre.

I want now to illustrate this and at the same time introduce a cross-cultural dimension to the discussion. Differences of poetic idiom are evident across time: the customary mode of composition and the aesthetic standards of verbal art, in, let us say, the eighteenth century are different from those of the Romantic period. But there are also differences across cultures at any one time. The poetic point of reference for the Japanese, for example, is likely to be the haiku rather than the sonnet or the ballad. How, then, does a haiku compare with the poems in the Western tradition which we have been dealing with so far?

It happens that there is a haiku which bears quite a close topical resemblance to the Frost poem *Dust of Snow* that we have been discussing.[18] In translation it goes like this:

Beauty

The usually hateful crow:
    he, too—this morning,
      on the snow!
(Matsuo Basho tr. Harold G. Henderson)

As we have seen, it is a feature of poetry in general that it does not make its meaning plain. We have to read between the lines. The haiku is particularly reticent, and provides very few lines for us to read between. It seems to be a sort of verbal distillation which represents the quintessence of an experience. One way of getting a feeling for its significance is to transpose it into a more familiar form. We have Frost's poem *Dust of Snow* at hand as a model for this purpose. So what would this haiku look like if it were to be remodelled in the Frost manner? What would be involved in the process? There would presumably have to be less reticence and particular readings between the lines would have to be written into the lines themselves, but without spelling them out. Here is one possibility:

Text F (Beauty)

The hateful crow
Is black on white
Against the snow
In morning light,

And makes me see,
This lovely day,
How things can be
In another way.

What observations might be made about this version? Inevitably, it verbalizes a particular interpretation of the original and in expanding on it reduces the range of its diversity of meaning. What, then, is foregrounded here? The contrast of black and white is brought out; the crow creates an effect of beauty associated with the light of early morning, in spite of its hateful self. It has a different being. Its association with the snow has a significance beyond appearances: it suggests another way of looking at things. Other versions would naturally give rise to other interpretations and other kinds of critical comment.

Having thus moved from an Eastern to a Western mode, we might next proceed in the reverse direction. What would the Frost poem look like if it were transposed into the form of a haiku? Instead of expanding the text we now have to reduce it, abstract out of it what we read as its essentials. Again, a variety of outcomes is possible. Here is one:

Text G (Dust of Snow)

A crow in a hemlock tree
  Shook down dust of snow—
    Reminding me!

What has been extracted from the Frost poem and what is the effect of the reformulation? The haiku version retains all the key lexical items of the first verse *(crow, hemlock tree, dust of snow)*. And its last line *(Reminding me!)* can be said to summarize some part of the second verse: what is described in the first verse does indeed remind the poet of something. Of what? Consider the possible significance of these lexical items: the (black) crow, eater of carrion, in a hemlock tree, suggestive of poison, shaking down dust (dust to dust) of snow, associated with winter, the dead season of the year. What the poet is reminded of, we might suggest, is his own mortality. And the haiku allows as much warrant for this interpretation as the original. What is left out is the changing of mood and the reverberation of familiar phrase and religious feeling (rue the day, save the day).

This process of poetic transposing, and discussion of its varied results, are intended to draw the attention of students not only to the particular features of Frost's poetry, but more generally to the difference of poetic idiom between the haiku and the short lyric of European tradition of the kind that I have been principally concerned with in this book. I want now to take this exercise in comparative literature a little further.

In the case of Frost's *Dust of Snow*, although, as we have seen, something is bound to be lost, the recasting into haiku-like form is relatively straightforward in that there is not all that much to reduce. But what if we were to deal with a longer poem? How would we proceed? There is a poem by Wordsworth, *The Solitary Reaper*, which is about a young girl singing alone in the fields as she is cutting grain. There is also, as it happens, a haiku by the Japanese poet Kobayashi Issa about a young girl singing alone in the fields as she is planting rice. Wordsworth's poem has thirty-two lines; Issa's has three. What is it that is said in the Wordsworth poem, one wonders, that takes ten times longer to say? How do the two poems compare? What is distinctive about their mode of representation?

Spring

In the thicket's shade,
　　and all alone, she's singing—
　　　　the rice-planting maid.
(Kobayashi Issa tr. Harold G. Henderson)

The Solitary Reaper

Behold her, single in the field,
Yon solitary Highland Lass!
Reaping and singing by herself;
Stop here, or gently pass!
5　Alone she cuts and binds the grain,
And sings a melancholy strain;
O listen! for the Vale profound
Is overflowing with the sound.

No Nightingale did ever chaunt
10　More welcome notes to weary bands
Of travellers in some shady haunt,
Among Arabian sands:
A voice so thrilling ne'er was heard
In spring-time from the Cuckoo bird,
15　Breaking the silence of the seas
Among the farthest Hebrides.

Will no one tell me what she sings?—
Perhaps the plaintive numbers flow
For old, unhappy, far-off things,
20　And battles long ago:
Or is it some more humble lay,
Familiar matter of to-day?
Some natural sorrow, loss, or pain,
That has been, and may be again?

25　Whate'er the theme, the maiden sang
As if her song could have no ending;
I saw her singing at her work,
And o'er the sickle bending;—
I listened, motionless and still;
30　And, as I mounted up the hill,
The music in my heart I bore,
Long after it was heard no more.
(William Wordsworth)

The task which students (with appropriate guidance) are to undertake is to gradually whittle the Wordsworth poem down to haiku shape through a series of reduced versions. This might seem to be a terrible thing to do to a work of art, murdering by dissecting (as Wordsworth himself put it) with a vengeance. But we shall see. Let us begin by first trying to edit it down to half its size, working from verse to verse, reducing each one from eight lines to four.

What, then, can we pare away from the first verse? We could start with the apostrophic expressions on the grounds that they do not actually contribute to the description itself. So *Behold her* goes, and *O listen!* and all of line 4. What else? Well, we might notice that as far as this description is concerned there is a good deal of redundancy. The title of the poem tells us that the reaper is solitary. We are told again four times in the first five lines: she is *single* (line 1), *solitary* (line 2), *by herself* (line 3), and *alone* (line 5). Indeed line 5 (together with the beginning of line 6) seems simply to repeat what is said in line 3: She is reaping and singing by herself, that is to say, alone she cuts and binds the grain and sings. To cut and bind grain is what the word 'reap' actually means. So there is surely some scope for reduction here. And do we need to know that this is a Highland Lass? Or that she is in a field (where else, after all, would she be reaping?). If we make all these verbal economies, what then do we come up with? Something like this:

> Alone she cuts and binds the grain,
> And sings a melancholy strain,
> And all around the vale profound
> Is overflowing with the sound.

We might pause at this stage to see what damage we have done, and conversely, of course, (and this is the point) to consider the significance of what we have excluded. What is the effect of the apostrophes of the original, for example? Is it that the poet is talking to himself, perhaps, drawing himself into participation, making the experience more immediate, less distanced as a third-person description? How would the redundancy fit into this? Perhaps this represents the process of reflection; perhaps he goes on about the solitariness of the reaper because he is trying to get some hold on the fleeting impression, trying to discover some significance in this lonely singing. Again, we may say that the effect is of immediacy, and this has disappeared in the reduced version. So what significance does he find? On to the second verse.

Here things get rather more difficult. There is less in the way of obvious redundancy to trim away. Perhaps we could dispense with the Arabian sands and the Hebrides (we have, after all, already got rid of the Highland Lass). That removes two of the eight lines straightaway. We know the cuckoo is a bird, and that its voice is heard in spring-time, so we could make economies in line 14. And do we need to be told that the nightingale sings, or *chaunts*, notes: if it welcomes weary travellers, how else could it do so other than by singing? And anyway the first verse has already established lonely singing as the theme. The birds too are presumably meant to be understood as solitary, though this is not mentioned. Why, then, do we need to mention the singing? After all this, what have we got left to render as a second verse: the nightingale welcoming weary travellers, and the cuckoo with its thrilling song breaking the silence of the seas. Arrange metrically and add in rhyme and we arrive at:

> No nightingale more welcome made
> To weary travellers in the shade.
> No cuckoo thrilled with notes like these,
> Breaking the silence of the seas.

This, it might be objected, is a poor substitute for the original, and so it is. But why? A dimension seems to have disappeared. The girl's singing in Wordsworth's poem opens up space and distance across sand and sea from Arabia to the farthest Hebrides, and this is represented in the very sound and rhythm of the verse. Our version confines it and there is little reverberation left.

So on to the next two verses. We have already established that the song is a melancholy strain, so we do not need *the plaintive numbers* in line 18. The battles mentioned in line 20 are an example of the *old, unhappy, far-off things* of line 19, so they can go as well. Lines 21 and 22 are glossed by the two lines which follow (the *natural sorrow* and so on are examples of the *familiar matter of to-day*), so perhaps they can be cut. As far as the last verse is concerned, the first four lines seem simply to restate what we know already: the maiden sings at her work. All we need to do here, perhaps, is to retain the last four lines. One moment, though. The maiden *sings*? *Sang*, surely. In verses 1 and 3 she sings in the present, but here in the fourth verse she sang in the past; and all the other verbs are in the past as well. Why then the shift in tense? Well, we are told that the music persists in the heart long after it is heard, so it *is* present as well as past, and the change in tense can be said to represent this. So the detachment of this last verse coexists with the immediacy of the first as two congruent and not contradictory perspectives on the same experience. If this is so, perhaps we can retain something of the significance of the original by keeping the last four lines with the change of tense, but excluding the first four. As a result of all these reductions, we might then come up with the following poetic précis:

> Alone she cuts and binds the grain,
> And sings a melancholy strain,
> And all around the vale profound
> Is overflowing with the sound.
>
> No nightingale more welcome made
> To weary travellers in the shade.
> No cuckoo thrilled with notes like these,
> Breaking the silence of the seas.
>
> Who knows the story that she sings?
> Of old, unhappy, far-off things?
> Familiar sorrow, loss or pain,
> That have been and may be again?
>
> I listened, motionless and still;
> And, as I mounted up the hill,
> The music in my heart I bore,
> Long after it was heard no more.

The next stage is to reduce these sixteen lines to eight. We could trim away the second two lines from the first verse to begin with, on the grounds that it is an incidental descriptive detail which is not subsequently developed. The sound of the singing reverberates away from the vale in the next verse. Here we have the invocations of the nightingale and the cuckoo. We could make do with just one of these birds: perhaps the cuckoo. So in this verse we could prune the first two lines. In the third verse, the first line seems superfluous. Why ask a question which is answered immediately afterwards? And the last line does not seem to add very much to the sense: it seems a little obvious to say that occasions for sorrow in the past are likely to recur in the future. So we are left with two lines. As it happens they do not rhyme, but it is not difficult to adjust them slightly so that they do. As to the last verse, we could get rid of the first two lines. We already know that he listened, and the fact that he was motionless and still (motionless *and* still?) does not seem to add anything of any significance. Nor, if it comes to that, does the fact that he mounted up the hill (how else would he mount if not up, one wonders). And so we cut our reduced poem down to half its size. It now looks like this:

> Alone she cuts and binds the grain,
> And sings a melancholy strain.
>
> No cuckoo thrilled with notes like these,
> Breaking the silence of the seas.
>
> Perhaps of loss and pain she sings,
> Or old, unhappy, far-off things.
>
> The music in my heart I bore,
> Long after it was heard no more.

What next? Is there any way of halving the poem again? Well, we could leave out the poet's excursions into imagination in verse 2 and into speculation in verse 3, leaving readers to imagine and speculate for themselves. We are then left with a simple four-line poem consisting of a brief description of a scene followed by a personal comment about its effect.

> Alone she cuts and binds the grain,
> And sings a melancholy strain.
> The music in my heart I bore,
> Long after it was heard no more.

But this, of course, still does not have the form, or the effect, of a haiku. What more do we need to do to fashion it into something resembling the Issa poem we started with? What seems to be distinctive about the haiku is that it represents an image, a third-person observation, and leaves its possible significance to be inferred. There seems to be a lack of any intrusive comment. This is what I meant earlier about its reticence. The last two lines of our final reduced version are first-person comment. If we want to convert it into something haiku-like, therefore, we need to get rid of them. If we then shape the first two lines so that they resemble a haiku form, we come up with something like this:

> She cuts and binds the grain,
>   all alone, and sings—
>   a melancholy strain.

This is no masterpiece. It is not really a haiku either if it comes to that (even though it measures the traditional seventeen syllables), since there are features of this mode of writing which cannot be captured in English. Apart from anything else (as was pointed out earlier) the visual effect of the written characters cannot be replicated in translation. Nevertheless, there it is with all its imperfections: a poem on a page. And as such it provokes interpretation, teases us into thought. Why so conclusively a *melancholy* strain? Is it because she cuts and binds the grain, gathers in a harvest? Is it because she is singing alone? What is it, then, that is significant about this image? The same sort of questions arise with this humble effort as they do with the original haiku by Issa.

One kind of significance is expressed in the Wordsworth poem from which this one has been abstracted, and which of course raises its own questions, as we have seen. The point is that the two poems have different effects, represent experience in different ways. It is the purpose of this activity to sharpen critical awareness of these differences of poetic idiom. And we might then go on to compare this derived haiku-like poem with the translation of the authorized one by Issa.

> In the thicket's shade,
>   and all alone, she's singing—
>   the rice-planting maid.

> She cuts and binds the grain,
>   all alone, and sings—
>   a melancholy strain.

We might observe that the two poems differ in that in one the focus of attention as expressed in the first line is on location whereas in the other it is on activity: the aloneness of the girl and her singing seems to be associated with where she is in the first case and with what she does in the second. In the Issa poem, the significance, as suggested by the noun phrase after the dash in the last line, would seem to centre on the maid, and in the other poem on the song she sings. Why, then, is the maid figured in this way in the first poem? What do the thicket's shade and the solitary singing contribute to the image? And, in the second poem, why is her song melancholy? Is it because she is alone, or because of the work she does, with its implications of autumn? The reticence of the poems invites a diversity of possible interpretation.

With Japanese students, of course, we could compare the translation with the original haiku, consider how far the rendering in English has the same representational effect, and invite students to produce their own versions which are in closer accord with the way they interpret the poem. Such activities naturally attract attention to the features of both languages, the different aspects of reality which they encode, and the limits they set on precision. Efforts at translating poetry bring home to us with particular force just how elusive significance is, and provide experience of the diversity and indeterminacy of meaning. But then all of the activities I have been proposing are designed to provide this experience. They could indeed be described as exercises in intralingual (as distinct from interlingual) translation, the deriving of one text from another with varying degrees of freedom.

14 In conclusion

In the case of the activities we have just considered, students would be drawn into cross-cultural comparison, relating familiar with unfamiliar forms of verbal art. But this principle is applicable in general to the kinds of text derivation and comparison which I have been demonstrating. In all cases students can be encouraged to compose and compare variants in styles most immediate to their experience, in the idiom, for example, of folk poetry, popular song, doggerel, or ribald rhyme. In this way, poetry which has been ennobled by tradition is made to rub shoulders with its humbler relations, and the common kinship is recognized. Is then nothing sacred? No. For when a poem becomes sacred, it shrivels to a relic.

We return to the points made in the first part of this book. The activities I have been proposing in this second part are their pedagogic application. They demystify poetry, democratize it indeed, by encouraging students to analyse it, read their own significance into it, rewrite it, make it their own. There is no place in this pedagogy for the ritualistic worship of canonized art. But nothing of value is denied to poetry by being irreverent about it. On the contrary, I would claim, it can lead to its value being recognized. The tragedy of King Lear is not diminished by the buffoonery of the Fool, but is enhanced by it. And in general, of course, this association of the high-flown and the down-to-earth, nobleness and vulgarity, the sacred and the profane, is common in all literature. One perspective on life presupposes the other. It seems entirely appropriate, therefore, that responses to poetry should act on such a presupposition. In reference to the lines of W.H. Auden cited earlier in the book, the pious fable keeps company with the dirty story, and the one can be a version of the other, setting off its significance.

Because of the aura of sanctity that so often surrounds it, poetry will provoke irreverence anyway. My point is that rather than seeking to suppress it, we can encourage it and make it serve the cause of understanding. But then it has to be *studied* irreverence, based on a close scrutiny of language and its effect, on an exploration of what I referred to earlier as its *poetentiality*. All of the activities I have suggested are intended to stimulate an enquiry into this, the ways in which different perspectives on reality are represented in poetry by the exploitation of the expressive possibilities of language.

Let me end with a last example. It is one which manipulates language in a particularly striking way after the manner of the concrete poetry which was discussed in an earlier chapter. It is not, I think, profound, nor by any means the greatest instance of verbal art. But although it is not especially illustrious, it is conveniently illustrative of that feature of poetry which I have been insisting on throughout these pages: the way in which the inherent possibilities of language are exploited to create new patterns of significance, new perspectives on familiar reality. At the same time, it will bring us back to the beginning of our discussion, provide a closure, and complete the pattern of this book.

one

t
hi
s

snowflake

(a
  li
    ght
  in
g)

is upon a gra

v
es
t

one

(e e cummings)

We return to the gravestones we started with: emblems of what

Philip Larkin calls 'the solving emptiness that lies just under all we do'. And lying just under all we do, and all we are, are the realities which cannot be socialized, which cannot be encompassed by the conventions of communal communication, but which can be expressed in the patterns of verbal art. They explain nothing. They solve nothing either. All the mysteries of experience and awareness remain unresolved, but at least we can feel attuned to them, if only fleetingly, and know something of ourselves. We can sense what things might mean beyond the limits of explanation.

Notes

1 (p.9) The question arises, of course, as to how far people are bound by this authorization. We may readily acknowledge that different languages encode different perspectives on reality. And it seems plausible enough to suppose that speakers are therefore disposed to see a world in terms of categories common to their community. This is the notion of linguistic relativity, which the work of Whorf has made familiar:

> We cut nature up, organize it into concepts, and ascribe significances as we do, largely because we are parties to an agreement to organize it in this way—an agreement that holds throughout our speech community and is codified in the patterns of our language.

Patterns of language are equated with patterns of thought: the agreement applies to both. But how binding is it? The text continues as follows:

> The agreement is, of course, an implicit and unstated one, *but its terms are absolutely obligatory*; we cannot talk at all except by subscribing to the organization and classification of data which the agreement decrees.
> (Whorf 1956: 215, emphasis in the original)

The argument slips easily from relativity to determinism. It is not simply that individuals in a community have a common conceptual disposition; they are constrained into conformity by the very code that they acquire. They have no choice: the terms are obligatory. This determinism (as a number of commentators have pointed out) is difficult to accept, and even more difficult to demonstrate. But it is a seductive doctrine. Fowler, for example, after quoting the passage above, comments:

Whorf's claim that language determines the categories of thought can be accepted so long as we qualify the argument somewhat: the semantic categories are not simply properties of the language, but products of the society in which the language is moulded.
(Fowler 1986: 32)

That is to say, individual thought is indeed determined by language, but by language as the agent of society. Individuals are socialized into communal ways of categorizing the world, then, and it is these social categories which are absolutely obligatory. You cannot conceive of any reality other than that which is linguistically encoded and so socially prescribed. In effect, individuality disappears. Later in this same book, Fowler appears to have second thoughts about his endorsement of the Whorf position. The hypothesis of linguistic determinism cannot, he says, be correct:

A language embodies way*s*, not *one way*, of looking at the world, and in these circumstances it is obvious that speakers are not going to be trapped within one overriding system of beliefs. Because speakers constantly make ideological shifts as they change modes of discourse ... they can experience a creative relativity of view.
(ibid. 149)

So relativity returns without determinism. But we should notice that speakers are still apparently constrained to adopt one system of beliefs or another. They cannot be unsystematic. Their creativity is a matter of shifting from one ideology, one set of communally shared values, to another. They move from conformity to conformity. They must always settle into some *social* position. My argument is that there are realities of individual awareness which must always elude such social categories, and that these realities, and their elusiveness, are what poetry (indeed, art in general) seeks to express.

2   (p.10)   The argument for the socialization of literature, which is currently in intellectual fashion, brings into convergence linguistic description and literary criticism. This is indicated by the title of the Fowler book mentioned earlier: *Linguistic Criticism*. The argument, essentially, is as follows. Human beings do not experience the world directly, but only

do so through categories which are encoded by their language and constitute the common sense of their communities. This is the relativity notion already referred to in Note 1. People's use of language, their discourse, is an expression of these linguistic and social categories, and so is a projection of a particular ideology. We shift next into determinism. Without these categories, Fowler tells us, hedging a little,

> ... it is doubtful whether we could think or communicate at all—we would be overwhelmed by individual impressions, unclassifiable and therefore incomprehensible.
> (Fowler 1986: 17)

In other words, since our way of classifying is that of our particular community, we cannot comprehend anything unless we can fit it into a communal classification. Individual impressions are meaningless unless and until they are transposed into social terms. All discourse is social action. *All* discourse. Literature is discourse, a use of language, so it inevitably conforms to the same social conditions as any other. Another book by Fowler, significantly enough, bears the title *Literature as Social Discourse* (Fowler 1981), and in it he makes his view of the non-distinctive nature of literature quite plain. Here is an expression of his position, quoted (with approval) in Carter and Simpson 1989:

> There is a dialectical interrelationship between language and social structure: the varieties of linguistic usage are both *products* of socio-economical forces and institutions—reflexes of such factors as power relations, occupational roles, social stratifications, etc., and *practices* which are instrumental in forming and legitimating these same social forces and institutions. The New Critics and the Formalists vehemently denied that 'literature' had social determinants and social consequences, but a sociolinguistic theory ... will show that *all* discourse is part of social structure and enters into ... effected and effecting relationships.
> (Fowler 1981: 21)

Literature, then, is a part of social structure and, like any other discourse, expresses established social categories. A poem is, in principle, no different from, say, a political pamphlet. Indeed, the inverted commas around the very term 'literature' in this quotation suggest that it can hardly be said to have any real identity at all. The literary theorist Terry Eagleton expresses just such a view in the concluding chapter of his book *Literary Theory*, entitled 'Political Criticism':

> My own view is that it is most useful to see 'literature' as a name which people give from time to time for different reasons to certain kinds of writing within a whole field of what Michel Foucault has called 'discursive practices', and that if anything is to be an object of study it is this whole field of practices rather than just those sometimes obscurely labelled 'literature'.
>
> (Eagleton 1983: 205)

Here the denial of the separate identity of literature is not only implicit in the inverted commas but explicitly stated. In defiance of semantics, Eagleton is saying that literary theory is emphatically not a theory of literature. It is a theory of discourse in general, discursive practices, or (in Fowler's terms) the practices which 'form and legitimate' social forces and institutions. Literary criticism is linguistic criticism. Its purpose is to examine how ideology is expressed, and control exerted, by means of socially determined discourses. A fine-grained study of the linguistic features of texts along these lines constitutes the new stylistics. Thus Fairclough's exercises in what he calls the 'critical discourse analysis' of newspaper articles (Fairclough 1989) is, in Eagleton's terms, an example of literary theory in practice. And this is not essentially different from the work on literary texts which appears in the book I referred to earlier (and published in the same year) which has the title *Language, Discourse and Literature: An Introductory Reader in Discourse Stylistics* (Carter and Simpson 1989). In the introductory chapter of this book we are told that the study of discourse along Eagleton/Fowler/Fairclough lines

> ... takes us beyond the traditional concern of stylistics with aesthetic values towards concern with the social and political ideologies encoded in texts.
>
> (Carter and Simpson 1989: 16)

As will be obvious, I take a very different view of these matters, indeed a diametrically opposite one. I do not believe that human life can be reduced by this kind of sociolinguistic accountancy to products and practices of socio-economic forces and institutions. There is also an unaccountable individual awareness of non-socialized reality, of a world which eludes conventional categorization but which is nevertheless comprehensible as other values in other terms. And it is these other terms, and these other values, aesthetic values indeed, that literature provides. Carter and Simpson seem to imply that a concern for such values is rather restrictive, and that we need to go 'beyond' them. But if this means that we investigate literature for traces of encoded social and political ideologies, then we do not go beyond but backwards by restricting literature to the confines of generalized and socially established convention. The position I argue in this book, then, is that literature is distinctive precisely because it cannot be socialized.

This point can be made in reference to the comments by Eagleton previously cited. Literature, he says, is just the 'name which people give from time to time for different reasons to certain kinds of writing'. But then the question arises as to what these reasons might be which impel people to distinguish certain kinds of writing as distinctive in some way. If people distinguish particular texts as different, they will read them differently. By the very argument on which Eagleton's position is based, which asserts that reality is what the language encodes, if people give the name of literature to a certain kind of writing, then it *is* literature, and they will respond to it accordingly. Over recent years poems have been displayed on London tube trains ('Poems on the Underground'). When I see one of these, I do not confuse it with the advertisements that keep it company. I identify it as distinctive and read it quite differently. I certainly do not scrutinize it to see what social and institutional ideologies it might be encoding.

For other discussions of poetry as social discourse, see Easthope 1983, Birch 1989.

3   (p.20)   But what if we were to reconstruct the actual historical circumstances of the poem's composition, and track

down the likely identity of this person with the lovely face? Would the phrase then take on a referential meaning for us? It would, I suggest, if the text were being used simply as documentary evidence and not read as a poem. Our interpretation does not depend on such biographical detection. If it did, the poem would be meaningless to those readers who could not make the contextual connection; that is to say, to all readers, except a tiny minority of researchers.

The point is that the interpretation depends on indeterminacy. This is a disadvantage for reference, since it is obviously inconvenient to be unclear about what people are talking about. But it is a necessary condition for representation, since it thereby provides for multiple meanings. Since a poem is severed from an association with any particular context, it can be interpreted in free association. Dislocated from the circumstances of composition, it can be relocated, so to speak, in the individual experience of the reader. So it is that poems are re-created on each occasion of their reading and relevance read into them by association with the particular reader's own world. The first- and second-person pronouns in poems, for example, continually change their values at different readings. They represent the participant roles of 'I' and 'you' without fixed incumbents: vacant identities for the reader to occupy. Consider, for example, these lines from a poem by Thomas Hardy:

Woman much missed, how you call to me, call to me,
Saying that now you are not as you were
When you had changed from the one who was all to me,
But as at first, when our day was fair.
(The Voice)

A note on this poem tells me that it was composed by Hardy in December 1912 and that his wife Emma Gifford had died the previous month. Are we to suppose, then, that the word 'woman' refers to her, and that Hardy is to be identified with the first-person 'I' and his wife with the second-person 'you'? If we treat this as a historical text, as a record of the past, yes. But as it is read, it is reactivated as present experience and the reader inhabits the first-person pronoun and invokes not Emma Gifford but some other second person. In other words, it represents experience and transcends the particular reference. All poems, I suggest, have transferable significance of this sort. This is why their meanings have no fixed location.

Readers might like to consider how they read themselves and their own experience into these lines by W.H. Auden:

> Lay your sleeping head, my love,
> Human on my faithless arm;
> Time and fevers burn away
> Individual beauty from
> Thoughtful children, and the grave
> Proves the child ephemeral:
> But in my arms till break of day
> Let the living creature lie,
> Mortal, guilty, but to me
> The entirely beautiful.
> *(Lay your sleeping head)*

Would it help, or hinder, representation and its transference effect if readers knew about the context of this poem's composition and could identify referentially who the participant persons in the poem actually were?

For further discussion of the distinction between reference and representation, and the contextual detachment or dislocation of literary discourse, see Widdowson 1975, 1984.

4   (p.25)   It might appear that in arguing that poetic texts are decontextualized representations of reality I am simply conforming to a conservative (and, for many, suspect) literary critical tradition which treats texts as revered icons with self-enclosed significance. But there is a crucial difference. In this tradition (at least according to Birch 1989), meanings are deemed to reside within the text, and interpretation therefore is a matter of recovering them. The process is, so to speak, a centripetal one: that is to say, the reader is drawn into the text by poetic forces, identifies its features from within, and so recognizes what the text means. In the account that I am proposing in this book, meaning is not a matter of recognition but of realization, not a matter of what a text means, but of what a text means to the reader. The process of interpretation is in this respect a centrifugal one: the poetic force, so to speak, throws out all manner of possible meanings. The very fact that the poem is dislocated from social context gives licence to

readers to locate its meaning in their own individual experience.

But how far does this licence run? Can we read anything we choose into the text? Is the text, indeed, nothing more than a pretext for the invention of meaning? Some critics, notably Stanley Fish, would seem to believe so:

> Interpretation is not the art of construing but the art of constructing. Interpreters do not decode poems; they make them.
>
> (Fish 1980: 327)

> No longer is the critic the humble servant of texts whose glories exist independently of anything he might do; it is what he does, within the constraints embedded in the literary institution, that brings texts into being and makes them available for analysis and appreciation. (ibid.: 368)

This would seem to suggest that for every poetic text there is a proliferation of poems, one for every individual reading, flying off centrifugally in all directions. But Fish imposes a control on such promiscuity by proposing that individual readers actually interpret in accordance with the norms of the 'interpretive communities' to which they belong (these are the 'constraints embedded in the literary institution'). As Scholes points out (in a telling criticism of Fish's position):

> The interpreter is freed from service to the text only to become the 'humble servant' of his ideological group.
>
> (Scholes 1985: 150)

Fish's proposal, then, leads again to the socialization of literature, whereby meanings are made to fit a particular ideological interpretation. It might also be noted that since the interpretive community of critics is likely to carry prestige, Fish in effect reinstates the notion of authoritative interpretation and so encourages the idea that the meaning of poetry (and literature in general) is a matter of expert exegesis, and that the student would be better advised to consult the secondary texts of literary criticism rather than the primary texts of literature itself. Indeed, since the critic actually *makes* poems, literary criticism in this view *is* the primary text. The approach that I take in this book is directly opposed to this. It is intended to encourage students to engage as individuals with poems as primary texts. For me, the crucial point about literature is that it provides the possibility of escape from institutional constraints, literary and otherwise.

For Fish, meaning is a matter of construction outside the text. For others, meaning is a matter of deconstruction inside the text: indeed outside the text there is nothing. This is the Derrida position: 'il n'y a pas de hors-texte' (Derrida 1967). The argument here, essentially, is that *all* texts are contextually disconnected and that interpretation is a process of endless deconstruction whereby we analyse one set of linguistic signs in terms of a different set, that set into another and so on *ad infinitum*, so that meaning is endlessly deferred by a succession of differences, and never engages with the extra-textual world. In this view, it is not possible for a text to mediate reference, because it makes no connections outside itself. And it cannot of course represent reality in the way I have suggested: decontextualization simply leads to recurrent deconstruction and we never break out from the bounds of the text.

One obvious way of countering this argument is to point to its very existence. The texts that Derrida and his adherents compose are *about* something; they refer to their own interpretative experience, their own conceptual world. If we constantly deconstructed in the way they suggest, we would never know what they were talking about. Indeed, it would not be proper to say that they were talking about anything, since to do so would be to arrest the endless and restless process of 'difference'. Of course it is the case that meanings are never textually fixed. But it is a social necessity, a condition on normal communication, that they should be stabilized by common agreement. We understand what the deconstructionists are saying because we suspend deconstruction and co-operate with them in the negotiation of meaning. This is a perfectly normal thing to do: we derive a discourse from the text. Of course, we can, abnormally, fixate on the text and deny it as discourse. We then enter into a state of textually induced trance where words suggest words suggest words suggest words in chain reactions of free association in total suspense from the real world of reference. This, it would appear, is what the deconstructionists do. They are essentially *entranced* by text. They get themselves into a mystical state of detached meditation on the meaning of language. But this is not a state which users of language can afford to be in. For them language has to be related to the world and used to achieve reference. For them it is a matter not of meditation but of mediation.

But what, one might ask, of representation? This, as I have argued, depends on disconnecting text from context, rather, it might seem, as deconstructionists propose. The essential point here is that disconnecting text from context does not involve disconnecting it from reality. On the contrary, my argument is that it allows for a fuller exploitation of the signifying potential of the language to express realities which are not conventionally encoded. We interpret meanings out of texts. Even the deconstructionists do this: the differences and deferrings which they identify are conditioned by their own particular dispositions, their own individual experiences of language and reality. And yet the meanings we read into texts are not independent of the texts themselves either. Interpretations must ultimately be referred back to the texts which activated them. There is a continual tension here between what is socially conventional in what texts mean and what the texts might mean for the individuals who interpret them. It is the recognition of this tension which is basic to the understanding of literature, and which, as I argue later, provides the rationale for the educational relevance of literary study.

My position here is consistent with that of Scholes:

> The position I take all along ... is that we neither capture nor create the world with our texts, but interact with it. Human language intervenes in a world that has already intervened in language. We divide the world into classes of things: trees, bushes, shrubs, flowers, weeds, and vegetables, for instance, which need not be divided up in just this way. But neither we as individuals, nor our cultural group, nor yet language itself can accomplish this division freely and arbitrarily. The world resists language as the grain of a tree resists the saw, and saws take the form they do partly because wood is what it is. We sense the presence of things through this resistance.
> (Scholes 1985: 111–12)

So neither Fish nor Derrida will do. We use our texts to

interact with the world, both that which is socially sanctioned and that which is individually apprehended. In other words, we interpret texts into discourses in different ways.

And here we come across another misapprehension (or so it seems to me), and one which relates to the points made in a previous note (Note 2) about the socialization of literature. In 1982 a book appeared entitled *Language and Literature: An Introductory Reader in Stylistics* (Carter 1982) and seven years later a companion volume was published with the title *Language, Discourse and Literature: An Introductory Reader in Discourse Stylistics* (Carter and Simpson 1989). The only difference in name between these volumes is the inclusion of the word *discourse* in the second. This implies that this aspect of language was not considered in the first, and indeed the introduction to the 1989 book would seem to bear out this implication, suggesting as it does that the first book was concerned only with the formal linguistic features of text. I was a contributor to the first book and this comes as a surprise to me, particularly since I had been at pains in a previous publication (Widdowson 1975) to define literature as discourse as the central concern of the stylistics I wished to practise. In fact, the first book is generally concerned with how literary texts can be interpreted, how texts can be used, in Scholes's terms, to interact with the world: they are about *readings* and how these can be activated and warranted by the linguistic features of the text. They are, in short, about discourse, just as this present book is. So how is the second volume different, and why should discourse figure now so prominently in the title? The main reason is that in the intervening years, the notion of discourse, including literary discourse, as social action has become fashionable and influential. The second book reflects the socialization of literature that I referred to earlier. The only discourse that it is now respectable to talk about is social discourse. In the introduction to the 1989 book, Carter and Simpson quote (with apparent approval) the view of Deirdre Burton that

> ... no analysis can be anything other than ideologically committed. Stylistic analysis is a political activity.
> (Carter and Simpson 1989: 8)

The second volume does not in fact extend the scope of

stylistics to include a discourse dimension missing in the first, because if by this is meant interpretation by readers interacting with the world by means of text, it was not missing in the first. There are, however, two things that it does do. Firstly, it redefines discourse in narrower terms to mean *ideologically committed* interpretation. And this, to my mind (as will be clear from previous comment in these notes), has the effect not of extending the scope of a stylistic analysis of literature, but of *reducing* it. Secondly, particularly in the chapters by Carter and Hoey, it shows how discourse can be directly derived from text by making overt the inter-activity, the presupposed dialogue, that is covertly present in all language use, and which can be activated in the process of interpretation. Engagement with a poem, as with any text, is an interactive process. There is always the implication of reaction: what do you mean? Why so? So what? Poems in this way stimulate the pragmatic process: the texts activate discourse in this sense.

Thus, the sort of interpretation that I, as a reader, have drawn out of the Yeats poem by interacting with it can be spelled out in terms of overt responses to the text, and these can be set down as protocols of a continuing exploration of meaning (see Short and van Peer 1989). For example:

One had a lovely face (who are you referring to?)
And one or two had charm (one or two *what?*)
(etc.)

In accordance with the procedure I have been practising of reformulating the poem to incorporate different possible interpretations, we might then write such responses into the text and come up with a version along the following lines:

One had a lovely face.
One who?
A girl in youth I used to know.
And one or two had charm.
Girls too.
But charm and face were in vain.
Why so?

Because the mountain grass
Cannot but keep the form
Where the mountain hare has lain.
You mean
That in the grass there is no trace
Where the hare has been?
Not so.
This is what I mean to say:
The grass, the charm, the lovely faces
Cannot help but keep their traces,
But traces cannot help but fade away.

For further discussion of deconstruction and interpretation
see Butler 1984, Culler 1983, Norris 1982, Scholes 1985.

5   (p.27)   This poem has often been cited as an example of
what might be called poetry of minimal artifice. It has obvious
parallels in the visual arts. There was an occasion some years
ago when a prize was awarded to an exhibit in the Tate
Gallery in London which consisted of a number of bricks
symmetrically stacked on the floor. Members of the public
were outraged: this was not art; it was just a pile of bricks. But
since the bricks were removed from their normal context (in a
builder's yard, for example), and presented in isolation,
framed, so to speak, by the gallery floor, they were no longer
just a pile of bricks. They drew attention to themselves and so
carried an implication of some other significance in their
appearance. The decontextualization and framing created the
conditions for art. One might object that if it is art, it is facile
and trivial and a travesty as compared with, say, Michelangelo
or Henry Moore. But although it may not be very highly
valued aesthetically, it is an instance of art form nevertheless.
It could not be an expression of any other kind.

The same point can be made about this poem by William
Carlos Williams. It is not just a note. It *cannot* just be a note,
any more than the bricks can just be bricks: its appearance
alters our perception of it. Consider in this connection the
following quotation from Butler and Fowler's collection of
'positions in literary theory' (Butler and Fowler 1971):

Can prose become poetry through typographical arrangement? I rather think it can. (Edwin Morgan: *The Times
Literary Supplement*, 28 January 1965)

Williams, then, we might say, has arranged a note as poetry.

But was there an actual note, one might wonder, which existed as a previous text? The editors of Williams's collected poems suggest that there was. They tell us that his wife, Florence, wrote a reply to *This Is Just to Say*, which the poet included alongside his own poem in one of his publications. They argue from this (by a process of reasoning I cannot myself follow) that the poem was indeed fashioned out of an actual note:

> Since WCW chose to include the reply in his own sequence it seems likely that he took a note left by his wife and turned it into a 'poem'.
> (Litz and MacGowan 1991: 536)

It would be interesting to compare (and to get students to compare) the way in which the notes are poetically rendered in each case. The Florence Williams text (as cited in Litz and MacGowan) runs as follows:

Reply

(crumpled on her desk)

Dear Bill: I've made a
couple of sandwiches for you.
In the ice-box you'll find
blue-berries—a cup of grapefruit
a glass of cold coffee.

On the stove is the tea-pot
with enough tea-leaves
for you to make tea if you
prefer—Just light the gas—
boil the water and put it in the tea

Plenty of bread in the bread-box
and butter and eggs—
I didn't know just what to
make for you. Several people
called up about office hours—

See you later. Love. Floss.

Please switch off the telephone.

It would generally be agreed, perhaps, that this is not a very inspired effort: banal and pedestrian are the terms that come most readily to mind. Unlike Williams's own text, we might say, it has no discernible pattern to it, and incites little curiosity. Nevertheless, since it is cast in the form of a poem, we are invited to read it as such and to realize its promise as representation by inferring some significance from it which does not directly declare itself. If it promises more than it delivers, and we cannot find such significance, then of course the poem fails.

Pedagogic treatments of the Williams poem (but not Florence's reply) appear in McRae and Pantaleoni 1986 and Maley and Duff 1989.

6   (p.32)   For a discussion of the co-operative principle, first proposed in Grice 1975, as providing the basic pragmatic ground rules for the negotiation of meaning in conversation, see Levinson 1983, Coulthard 1985. An application of the principle for the analysis of drama appears in Burton 1980, Downes 1988, Short 1989.

7   (p.41)   The phenomenon of present/past tense alternation is, of course, common in informal spoken narrative. Quirk *et al.* (1985) provide an example of it when illustrating the use of the 'historic' present for talking about past events:

> I couldn't believe it! Just as we arrived, up comes Ben and slaps me on the back as if we're life-long friends . . .

And they comment:

> The historic present describes the past as if it is happening now: it conveys something of the dramatic immediacy of an eye-witness account.
> (Quirk *et al.* 1985: 181)

In other words (in my words), the event is *represented*. It takes on the features of fiction.

By the same token, we might argue that Coleridge is representing the encounter of the mariner and the wedding-guest in a similar dramatic eye-witness way, and I would concede that the reader can respond to that without drawing out implications about the ambivalent existence of the mariner, as I go on to do in the analysis that follows. There is, after all, nothing particularly ambivalent, one supposes, about the world that Ben inhabits in the example quoted above from Quirk *et al.* As always, literary representation allows for the assignment of significance at different levels of interpretation.

But if the tense alternation is to be read as a dramatic device for achieving immediacy, the effect seems to be counteracted by Coleridge's use of marginal commentary throughout the poem. Alongside the opening verse, for example, we find the gloss, in prose (and in the present tense):

> An ancient Mariner meeteth three gallants bidden
> to a wedding feast, and detaineth one.

It is not at all obvious how this commentary is to be understood. Apart from the poetic text as such, it is nevertheless in close attendance, and it is presumably meant to be read alongside the poem as a continual accompaniment. Shifting too between past and present tenses, it is sometimes quite elaborate in content, sometimes couched in curious archaic style. Its effect is not to make the narrative more immediate but to put it at a further remove, set it in an extra frame and so to provide it with another dimension of reality or (equally) of illusion. It is like double exposure indirect speech.

8   (p.47)   One of my reasons for considering these lines is that they are discussed by William Empson in *Seven Types of Ambiguity*, and the reader might wish to refer to his analysis. Empson makes the following comment on the process of interpretation:

> Lacking rhyme, metre, and any overt device such as comparison, these lines are what we should normally call poetry only by virtue of their compactness; two statements are made as if they were connected, and the reader is forced to consider their relations for himself. The reason why these facts should have been selected for a poem is left for him to invent; he will invent a variety of reasons and order them in his own mind. This, I think, is the essential fact about the poetical use of language.
> (Empson 1961: 24–5)

The inference of connection, however, is the essential fact about *all* uses of language and is not distinctive of poetry. It is a very general feature of interpretation that we consider the relations between expressions so as to infer meanings pragmatically which have not been overtly signalled by linguistic means. This is the point of the co-operative principle: language users assume that the words they use will be referred to the shared maxims of communicative interaction, and to common contextual knowledge. Consider, for example, the following two expressions (adapted from Sperber and Wilson 1986); a question followed by a reply:

A: Would you like to buy a flag?
B: I always spend my holidays in Birmingham.

B here is making a statement without any overt linguistic device which can connect it with A's question, but we assume that some connection is to be inferred, that B's utterance is related to A's question and is indeed meant to be a relevant response. But what *is* the connection? A little additional contextual information will help.

The first utterance is from somebody selling flags to raise funds for the Royal National Lifeboat Association. The second utterance is from a passerby. Birmingham is a town in the midlands of England, away from the seaside. So we might infer that B's reply is intended as a refusal to give money on the grounds that he will not benefit from any service which the Lifeboat Association might provide. Once we can locate the two expressions as question and reply in a particular context, we can home in on their relationship, and thus arrive at a conclusive interpretation: this is what B must mean. But the two statements in the lines of the poem cannot be so located. They are associated with each other but not contextually connected. We do not know who is speaking, whether there is one voice or two; we have no time and place co-ordinates to refer the expressions to. In the case of the flagseller and the passerby, contextual information provides us with evidence which enables us to *discover* the connection. Without such evidence, the reader will *invent* a variety of possible connections, without being able to settle into a conclusive one. Here, then, is the distinctive feature of poetic interpretation: not that the reader will be forced to consider the relations between expressions whose connection is not explicitly signalled, for that is a general pragmatic requirement for all interpretation, but that these relations will necessarily be, in the absence of contextual evidence, a matter of invention, and so intrinsically indeterminate. Poetic meanings do not settle.

The same point can be expressed in terms of relevance theory, as expounded in the Sperber and Wilson book referred to earlier. They talk about the relative determinacy of implicatures. Strong implicatures, with a high degree of determinacy, are those which the hearer is encouraged to recognize as intended. This recognition depends, clearly, on the invocation of a shared context. They provide the following example:

Peter: Would you drive a Mercedes?
Mary: I wouldn't drive ANY expensive car.
(Sperber and Wilson 1986: 194)

For Peter to hear Mary's remark as coherent, that is to say as a relevant reply to his question, he has to recognize that she intends him to refer to their assumed shared knowledge that a Mercedes is an expensive car, and to conclude that she would not drive one. If he does not pick up on this implicature, the interaction founders.

But there are, of course, cases where speaker intention is not so easy to identify, and where the utterance, therefore, can give rise to a wide range of weak or indeterminate implicatures of the hearer's own devising: in other words, the implicatures are not discovered but invented. This activation of weak implicatures, this indeterminate invention, Sperber and Wilson call (significantly enough) the *poetic effect*. They provide the following example:

> Mary came with Peter, Joan with Bob, and Lily with a sad smile on her face.

And they comment as follows:

> ...the hearer's task is to find a set of assumptions in the context of which the facts that Mary came with Peter, Joan with Bob, and Lily with a sad smile on her face have either identical or directly contrasting implications. What might be suggested is that Lily had no one to come with, that she was sad because she had no one to come with, that there was a whole story behind her sad smile in which Mary, Peter, Joan and Bob were somehow involved, and which an imaginative hearer could spell out along a whole variety of lines.
> (Sperber and Wilson 1986: 223–4)

These comments have themselves an intertextual echo. They can be taken as the expression, in different terms, of what Empson is talking about. The name he gives to the feature of poetic texts which gives rise to this indeterminate and divergent range of implicatures is ambiguity. The point I would wish to stress with regard to my own argument in this book is that these poetic effects arise as a result of contextual dislocation, when the hearer/reader cannot recover or discover the context of the speaker/writer and so has to create his own, thereby assuming himself the responsibility of relevance.

There is a further observation to be made about Empson's discussion of these two lines of verse: a matter which arises from the textual status, so to speak, of the lines themselves. Empson refers to them as 'an example from one of Mr Waley's Chinese translations'. I had always assumed (in common, I imagine, with other readers) that the two lines constituted a complete poem. But Jennifer Bassett has pointed out to me that this is not the case at all; that they are in fact only a fragment, the first two lines of an eight-line poem by T'ao Ch'ien which, in Waley's translation, runs as follows:

New Corn

Swiftly the years, beyond recall.
Solemn the stillness of this fair morning.
I will clothe myself in spring-clothing
And visit the slopes of the Eastern Hill.
By the mountain-stream a mist hovers,
Hovers a moment, then scatters.
There comes a wind blowing from the south
That brushes the fields of new corn.

Empson, then, is only giving us part of a poem, but even that part is textually inaccurate: Waley has *fair* morning, and not, as Empson has it, *spring* morning. We might surmise that the word has been transferred in Empson's mind from the following line, and that he is quoting from memory. And this is borne out by the fact (also pointed out by Jennifer Bassett) that he cites actual words from the rest of the poem in his discussion of the effect of these opening lines, and again misquotes. This is the relevant passage:

... the *years* of a man's life seem *swift* even on the small scale, like the mist from the mountains which 'gathers a moment, then scatters'.
(Empson 1961: 24)

Gathers, we note, not, as in the original, *hovers*.

What are we to make of this? It might be suggested that Empson, himself both poet and sinologist, was familiar with the Chinese text and changed the Waley rendering deliberately to make it accord with his own interpretation of the original. Alternatively (and this seems more likely), he is (mis)quoting the Waley text from memory. But in either case, what is exemplified here is the way Empson, like any reader, interprets meaning out of poem and makes it his own in an alternative version. This is the point of importance for the argument of this book. What counts is what we *make* of poems.

By the same token, the fact that these two lines are a textual fragment does not invalidate interpretations based on the assumption that they constitute the whole. If we read them as a complete poem, they *are* a complete poem. We read them apart. What is of interest is how differently we then interpret the lines when we read them not apart from but as a part of the rest of the poem. This suggests that one (of many) activities which might be devised, at an appropriate level, to complement and extend those proposed in the second part of this book would be to present students with poetic fragments as if they were complete, and then get them to reconsider their interpretations when these fragments are fitted back into the original texts.

9   (p.55)   Thus Culler:

A major point on which there would be agreement ... is that literary works are to be considered not as autonomous entities, 'organic wholes', but as intertextual constructs: sequences which have meaning in relation to other texts which they take up, cite, parody, refute, or generally transform. A text can be read only in relation to other texts ...
(Culler 1981: 38)

For Beaugrande and Dressler, intertextuality is one of seven standards of textuality in general. As they point out

(Beaugrande and Dressler 1981: Chapter IX), there are two aspects to it. One is the relationship of a particular text to a type or genre. When we come across a piece of writing, part of our interpretation depends on our recognition of what conventions it conforms to as a text type. So we read a poem in a particular way because we identify it as a poem. My general purpose in this book is to consider, in the case of the short lyric poem, just such typical features, and the effect they have on interpretation. The second aspect is the relationship between particular texts: what Beaugrande and Dressler refer to as text allusion. This is when there are verbal echoes, a deliberate or unintentional invocation of actual wording. It is this allusive aspect of intertextuality that I am talking about in this chapter.

The example of allusive intertextuality that Beaugrande and Dressler provide is the series of variants written by Ralegh, Donne, and Day Lewis on Marlowe's poem *The Passionate Shepherd to His Love* ('Come live with me and be my love ...'). The procedure I have adopted throughout this book as a general principle of interpretation is, of course, one which produces deliberate variations of this kind.

But as I indicate in my discussion, the difficulty with allusive intertextuality is to know when it is reasonable to suppose that there is an intended allusion, and the extent to which our interpretation depends on recognizing it. Perhaps I might give a further example here—one which falls outside the scope of my concern in this book with the short lyric.

The last act of Shakespeare's *The Merchant of Venice* opens with a set of speeches by the lovers Lorenzo and Jessica, which create the magical ambience of the moonlight scene at Belmont:

LORENZO

    The moon shines bright. In such a night as this,
    When the sweet wind did gently kiss the trees,
    And they did make no noise; in such a night,
    Troilus, methinks, mounted the Trojan walls,
    And sigh'd his soul toward the Grecian tents,
    Where Cressid lay that night.

JESSICA   In such a night
Did Thisbe fearfully o'ertrip the dew,
And saw the lion's shadow ere himself,
And ran dismay'd away.
LORENZO   In such a night ...

And so on. 'In such a night ...' recurs as a refrain, like an incantation. Now exactly the same phrase occurs in the mouth of another character in Shakespeare, on another night, but a very different one. It is the night when Lear is turned out into the storm:

LEAR   Filial ingratitude!
Is it not as this mouth should tear this hand
For lifting food to't? But I will punish home.
No, I will weep no more.—*In such a night*
To shut me out! Pour on; I will endure.
In such a night as this!

Are we to invoke these verbal echoes when interpreting each scene? Are we to superimpose the placid moonlight of Belmont on the massive turbulence of the storm? Does it indeed matter if nobody has ever noticed the intertextual correspondence? Once it has been pointed out, we can always, of course, assign significance to it. One might, for example, point out that both scenes follow on from acts of filial betrayal in which a daughter deprives the father of the very things which sustain his self-respect. On the one hand we see the happy consequences for the daughter; on the other the disastrous consequences for the father. The first belongs to comedy, the second to tragedy. In this respect we can interpret the two plays as variations on a theme.

It is not difficult to develop a quite elaborate interpretative construction on an intertextual correspondence of this kind; or indeed of any kind, since there is no limit to ingenuity. There are intertextual correspondences between almost all texts simply by virtue of the fact that they are written in the same language. The problem is to know which ones are relevant for interpretation and which are not. As Stanley Fish points out:

> If one sets out to describe in the absence of that which marks out the field of description (the experience of the reader), there is no way of deciding either where to begin or where to stop, because there is no way of deciding what counts. In such a situation, one either goes on at random and forever (here we might cite the monumental aridity of Jakobson's analyses of Baudelaire and Shakespeare) or one stops when the accumulated data can be made to fit a preconceived interpretive thesis.
> (Fish 1980: 94–5)

Fish is referring here to the fine-grained structuralist analysis to be found in Jakobson and Levi-Strauss (1962), Jakobson and Jones (1970), whereby intricate connections across patterns of linguistic equivalences are identified *within* a particular text. My point is that Fish's comment applies equally to the proliferation of possible connections which a reader might make *across* texts. Invoking the reader does not solve the problem. Indeed, if one accepts the view of relevance theory and its definition of poetic effect (as discussed in the previous note), such proliferation is a necessary consequence of literary uses of language which leave the reader with the responsibility for inferring weak implicatures. It is of course a problem for reference. But for representation it is an essential condition.

Another issue that arises from intertextuality (as the example from Shakespeare indicates) is the extent to which the particular interpretation of a poem depends on transferring significance from other poems by the same author. In some cases, of course, poems are written in sets or sequences so that such transference is induced by design. But even when a poem appears as a one-off piece, readers will naturally tend to relate it thematically to the writer's other work they may know. If, for example, we were to read Yeats's poem *Memory* in association with other poems of his which express a sense of the power of primitive nature (as in *A Prayer for My Daughter, The Wild Swans at Coole*, the Crazy Jane poems, and so on), then we might come up with an interpretation very different from those I have proposed earlier. Thus, in his comments on an earlier draft of this book, Alan Maley makes the following suggestion:

With regard to the Yeats poem *Memory*, I wonder if another interpretation might be offered? It would go something like this:

> *lovely/charm* suggest a civilized existence
> *mountain grass/hare* suggest the savage, the primitive, the untamed.

The paraphrase would then go somewhat thus: 'I have met charming, lovely civilized women (?) but they meant nothing to me so I've forgotten them. The only one I really recall is the wild woman whose nature matched my own.'

10 (p.78) It is this *poetentiality* which Seamus Heaney seems to be talking about in his inaugural lecture as the Oxford Professor of Poetry entitled *The Redress of Poetry*. What he calls the impulse of poetry is to:

> place a counter-reality in the scales, a reality which is admittedly only imagined but which nevertheless has weight because it is imagined within the gravitational pull of the actual. This redress of poetry comes from its being a revelation of potential that is denied or constantly threatened by circumstances.
> (Heaney 1990: 4)

Later in the lecture, he expresses (with more eloquence than I can command) the significance, the poetentiality, of poetry that I have argued for in this book by saying that it 'gives voice and retaliatory presence to suppressed life' (Heaney 1990: 7). Just so.

11 (p.90) For example, Carter and Long 1987, Duff and Maley 1990. A particularly comprehensive and impressive demonstration of these activities appears in Maley and Duff 1989, which deals exclusively with the teaching of poetry. For a survey of recent developments in the teaching of literature in English overseas see Lott 1988. For a review of work on stylistics and literature teaching in general see Short 1990.

12 (p.91) See in particular McRae 1991. McRae takes up the distinction between reference and representation that I have made here and elsewhere (e.g. Widdowson 1975, 1984) but defines the terms somewhat differently. For him representational language is that which engages the imagination,

whether it is counted as literary or not:

> Representational language opens up, calls upon, stimulates and uses areas of the mind, from imagination to emotion, from pleasure to pain, which referential language does not reach. Where referential language informs, representational language involves.
> (McRae 1991:3)

His book suggests ways of using examples of representational language (literature with a small 'l', as he calls them) to provide priming for literary understanding by language awareness.

13 (p.121)   These passages are quoted in a book edited by Lyn Macdonald entitled *They called it Passchendaele: The story of the Third Battle of Ypres and of the men who fought in it*. Part 5 of the book has the title (with inverted commas) '*We Died in Hell—They Called it Passchendaele*'. It is interesting, however, that no indication is given that the title is a quotation from a poem by Sassoon.

> Squire nagged and bullied till I went to fight,
> (Under Lord Derby's Scheme). I died in hell—
> (They called it Passchendaele) . . .
> (Siegfried Sassoon: *Memorial Tablet*)

14 (p.139)   The original compendium of curiosities was edited by Charles Hindley and published in 1871 by Reeves and Turner. The passages here are taken from a reprint in Sola Pinto and Rodway 1965.

15 (p.149)   In this activity I have suggested that an authorized text can be compared with a derived one. But one can also find versions for comparison which are authorized as the poet's early and later drafts of the 'same' poem, and which in some cases have actually appeared in print. This is particularly the case, as it happens, with William Carlos Williams. He has a way of retaining different versions, so it is not that one supersedes the other as a revision: they both coexist as variants on a theme. This being so, we might follow the activity discussed here with one which asks students to compare two authorized variants from Williams's work. For example:

The Locust Tree in Flower

[First Version]

Among	Among
the leaves	of
bright	green
green	stiff
of wrist-thick	old
tree	bright
and old	broken
stiff broken	branch
branch	come
ferncool	white
swaying	sweet
loosely strung—	May
come May	again
again	
white blossom	

clusters
hide
to spill

their sweets
almost
unnoticed

down
and quickly
fall

16 (p.158)   An analysis of this poem appears in Cluysenaar 1976.

17 (p.166)   The reader might wish to consider how far the discussion of this poem here complements the treatment of it in Widdowson 1975.

18 (p.169)   I am not alone in noticing the resemblance. Claire Kramsch has drawn my attention to a paper presented by Masako Hiraga at Cornell University entitled 'Snow and Crow: Basho's haiku in comparison with Robert Frost's short poem in an advanced Japanese classroom' (see Kramsch forthcoming).

Appendix

I provide here sets of texts which readers might themselves wish to compare along the lines suggested in the analyses of Part Two. Texts A–D relate to Chapter 11, texts E–L to Chapter 12. Since readers might wish to decide for themselves which are the authorized and which the derived poems, I have delayed information on authorship to a later page.

A: Ozymandias

Text 1

A traveller from an antique land once told me that in the desert there stand two vast legs of stone. There is no body, but near those legs, half buried in the sand there is a shattered face of stone, with a frown and a wrinkled lip, a kind of cold, commanding sneer. And these words appear on the pedestal: 'My name is Ozymandias, king of kings. Look on my works, ye Mighty, and despair.' Nothing remains beside the ruin. Boundless and bare, round the decay of that colossal wreck, the lonely level sands stretch far away into the distance. Nothing is left of Ozymandias and his works but this ruin. This might make us despair, but for another reason, perhaps, than the one he himself had in mind.

Text 2

I met a traveller from an antique land
Who said: Two vast and trunkless legs of stone
Stand in the desert . . . Near them, on the sand,
Half sunk, a shattered visage lies, whose frown,
And wrinkled lip and sneer of cold command,
Tell that its sculptor well those passions read
Which yet survive, stamped on these lifeless things,
The hand that mocked them and the heart that fed:

And on the pedestal these words appear:
'My name is Ozymandias, king of kings:
Look on my works, ye Mighty, and despair!'
Nothing beside remains. Round the decay
Of that colossal wreck, boundless and bare
The lone and level sands stretch far away.

Text 3

Two vast and trunkless legs of stone
Stand in the desert; in the sand,
Half sunk, a shattered face with frown
And wrinkled lip of cold command.

And on the stone these words appear:
'Ozymandias, king of kings.
Look on my works and then despair!'
Nothing remains but ruined things.

Around the wreck that's lying there
Nothing remains. Round the decay
Of ruin, lonely, boundless, bare,
The level sands stretch far away.

B: Faintheart in a Railway Train

Text 1

The journey was a tedious one and I looked listlessly out of the
train window. Time went by; hour followed hour. At nine o'clock
in the morning we passed a church. At ten, there was the sea. At
twelve we came to a town, grey and grimy, full of smoke and
smirch. And after that, at two, we passed a forest of oak and birch
trees. And then, on a platform, there she was: a radiant stranger
standing there on a platform. She was not aware of me. She did
not see me looking at her. I thought to myself: 'Do I dare to get out
here, talk to her?' But I kept my seat, waiting for some reason,
some purpose or plea which would justify the action. And then the
wheels moved and the moment was gone. If only, if only it could
have been otherwise. If only I had alighted there. But the train
moved on, and I never saw her again.

Text 2

Hour after hour the train moved, past a church
At one time, at another past the sea,
Then past a grey town, grimy in its smoke,
Then green trees of a forest, birch and oak,
    Then, on a platform, she:

A radiant stranger, unaware of me.
I thought: 'Now why not get down from the train
And meet her?' But I waited. Suddenly
Wheels moved. The train went by her. She
    Never came to my sight again.

Text 3

At nine in the morning there passed a church,
At ten there passed me by the sea,
At twelve a town of smoke and smirch,
At two a forest of oak and birch,
    And then, on a platform, she:

A radiant stranger, who saw not me.
I said, 'Get out to her do I dare?'
But I kept my seat in my search for a plea,
And the wheels moved on. O could it but be
    That I had alighted there!

C: My life closed twice ...

Text 1

My life came to an end in the past at moments of parting, so it has
closed twice already before its actual close in death. It remains to
be seen if after death, in immortality, I shall experience the same
kind of event that I have already experienced before, as overwhelming and as hopeless: another parting to be looked back at
with regret.

Text 2

My life, in pangs of parting,
Has ended twice before.
And will there be a third event
To make me suffer more?

Such hopelessness of parting
That I have suffered so
Tells everything of hell we need,
And all of heaven we know.

Text 3

My life closed twice before its close.
It yet remains to see
If immortality unveil
A third event to me,

So huge, so hopeless to conceive
As these that twice befell.
Parting is all we know of heaven,
And all we need of hell.

Text 4

My life closed with two partings
From those I see no more.
So will the close of life then be
A parting as before?

Will I from immortality
Look backwards with regret,
And think of those I left behind,
Unable to forget?

Text 5

My life closed twice already,
And what these partings show
Is everything of hell we need,
And all of heaven we know.

D: Tall Nettles

Text 1

As they have done in the spring for many years now, tall nettles cover up the debris of old farm implements in this corner of the farmyard—the worn-out plough, the rusty harrow, the roller made of stone. The nettles are so tall that only the butt of the elm tree now tops them. I like this place. It appeals to me strongly for some reason. I like the dust on the nettles as much as the bloom on flowers. The dust is always there on the nettles, except just after a shower of rain. But then this just seems to prove how sweet the shower is, to show the pleasure of present experience, the living moment set against the dust and dereliction of the past. The bloom on the flower and the dust on the nettles both seem to tell us of time passing, past and present, growth and decay, and how the one is implied by the other.

Text 2

Tall nettles cover up, as they have done
These many springs, the rusty harrow, the plough
Long worn out, and the roller made of stone:
Only the elm butt tops the nettles now.

This corner of the farmyard I like most:
As well as any bloom upon a flower
I like the dust on the nettles, never lost
Except to prove the sweetness of a shower.

Text 3

The worn-out plough, the roller made of stone,
The rusty harrow, other farm debris,
Are covered up by nettles that have grown
Over the years. This place appeals to me.

Dust on the nettles, like bloom on a flower,
Tells of time passing. When it's washed away,
It proves to me the sweetness of a shower,
The freshness of the present in decay.

Text 4

Tall nettles hide
The rusty plough.
Only the elm butt
Tops them now.

Dust on their leaves
Always remains—
Save in the freshness
When it rains.

E: So we'll go no more a-roving

Text 1

We'll go no more a-roving
  By the light of the moon,
Though the night was made for loving,
  And the day returns too soon.

For the sword outwears its sheath,
  And the soul wears out the breast,
And the heart must pause to breathe,
  And love itself have rest.

So we'll go no more a-roving
  So late into the night,
Though our hearts are still as loving
  And the moon is still as bright.

Text 2

So, we'll go no more a-roving
  So late into the night,
Though the heart be still as loving
  And the moon be still as bright.

For the sword outwears its sheath,
  And the soul wears out the breast,
And the heart must pause to breathe,
  And love itself have rest.

Though the night was made for loving,
  And the day returns too soon,
Yet we'll go no more a-roving
  By the light of the moon.

F: Love without Hope

Text 1

Love without hope, as when the young bird-catcher
Swept off his tall hat to the squire's own daughter.
So let the imprisoned larks escape and fly
Singing about her head, as she rode by.

Text 2

The young bird-catcher loved apart,
And caught birds with a heavy heart.
Remote his object of desire:
He loved the daughter of the squire.

It happened that they met one day.
He tried to think of words to say,
Abashed at such a sudden meeting;
He swept his tall hat off in greeting.
The birds escaped, sang round her head.
But she rode off. No words were said.

G: 'Me up at does'

Text 1

Me up at does

out of the floor
quietly Stare

a poisoned mouse

still who alive

is asking What
have i done that

You wouldn't have

Text 2

One day I found, in my house,
On the floor, a poisoned mouse,
Still alive. Its staring eye
Seemed to ask me: What have I
Done to deserve this agony
You would not do if you were me?
A question that has no reply.

H: Heaven-Haven

Text 1

I have asked to go
Where no springs fail,
Where fields are free of sharp and sided hail,
And a few lilies blow.

I have desired to be
Where storms not come
To havens where swells stay not disturbed and dumb,
And out of the swing of the sea.

Text 2

I have desired to go
Where springs not fail,
To fields where flies no sharp and sided hail
And a few lilies blow.

And I have asked to be
Where no storms come,
Where the green swell is in the havens dumb,
And out of the swing of the sea.

Text 3

I have a longing now to go
To fields where a few lilies blow,
To fields all free of driving hail,
To fields where warm springs do not fail.

I have a longing now to be
Out of the swinging of the sea,
Where the swell is in the havens dumb,
And all is still, and no storms come.

I: Mother of the Groom

Text 1

What she remembers
Is his glistening back
In the bath, his small boots
In the ring of boots at her feet.

Hands in her voided lap,
She hears a daughter welcomed.
It's as if he kicked when lifted
And slipped her soapy hold.

Once soap would ease off
The wedding ring
That's bedded forever now
In her clapping hand.

Text 2

She thinks now of the child that he was then,
Peering from his pram along the street,
Sitting in the bath, his glistening back,
A pair of small boots lying by her feet.

She sits there, clasped hands in her empty lap,
And hears a daughter welcomed to the fold.
It feels as if, when lifted up he kicked,
And slipped forever from her soapy hold.

She looks down at her hands. The wedding ring
Could be eased off with soap once, set aside,
But now it is embedded in the skin
Of the clapping hand that greets the groom and bride.

J: Mind

Text 1

The mind is like a bat
That beats in caves alone,
Contriving by its wit
To avoid the walls of stone.

Not needing to explore,
It knows what rock is there,
And so may dip and soar
Across the blackest air.

So should one then accept
This simile? Yes, save
That errors can correct
The nature of the cave.

Text 2

Mind in its purest play is like some bat
That beats about in caverns all alone,
Contriving by a kind of senseless wit
Not to conclude against a wall of stone.

It has no need to falter or explore;
Darkly it knows what obstacles are there,
And so may weave and flitter, dip and soar
In perfect courses through the blackest air.

And has this simile a like perfection?
The mind is like a bat. Precisely. Save
That in the very happiest intellection
A graceful error may correct the cave.

Text 3

Free playing of the mind is like the flight
Of a bat that flutters in a cave alone,
Sensing by instinct, without sense of sight,
How to avoid decisive walls of stone.

So the mind is free to range on bat-like wings,
Unhindered by the obstacles there,
It dips and soars in freedom, swoops and swings
In perfect courses by instinctive flair.

And is this simile perfection too?
The resemblance is false in one respect.
Bats do not change their confines, but minds do,
And caves are carved out by the intellect.

K: As Bad as a Mile

Text 1

I hold the apple in my palm.
I eat the apple to the core,
Then aim it, lifting up my arm;
But miss the basket with my throw.
I see it skid across the floor:
Just missed. Bad luck. And yet I know

That there is failure here, some lack
Marked earlier in the moves before,
Failure that I feel spreading back
Up the muscles of the arm
To the hand and fingers, as once more
I hold the apple in my palm.

Text 2

I eat the apple and I shy the core:
It hits the basket, skids across the floor.
I missed my aim. Bad luck, and nothing more.

Yet I sense failure spreading up the arm,
Further and earlier, the hand unraised and calm,
The apple unbitten in the palm.

Text 3

Watching the shied core
Striking the basket, skidding across the floor,
Shows less and less of luck, and more and more

Of failure spreading back up the arm
Earlier and earlier, the unraised hand calm,
The apple unbitten in the palm.

L: The Eagle

Text 1

He clasps the crag with crooked hands;
Close to the sun in lonely lands,
Ringed with the azure world, he stands.

The wrinkled sea beneath him crawls;
He watches from his mountain walls,
And like a thunderbolt he falls.

Text 2

He stands close to the sun on high,
Watching the world below go by,
Ringed with the blue world of the sky.

He grips the rock and looks below
To the dark sea's endless ebb and flow.
Then shoots like an arrow from a bow.

Text 3

He clasps the crag
With crooked hands,
Close to the sun
In lonely lands.

He watches from
His mountain walls;
The wrinkled sea
Beneath him crawls;

And like a thunderbolt
He falls.

(The reader might wish to compare these versions of *The Eagle* with those presented in Maley and Duff 1989. This poem is also discussed in Carter and Long 1987.)

Authors of the original poems in the appendix

A: *Ozymandias* Percy Bysshe Shelley
B: *Faintheart in a Railway Train* Thomas Hardy
C: *My life closed twice* ... Emily Dickinson
D: *Tall Nettles* Edward Thomas
E: *So we'll go no more a-roving* Lord Byron
F: *Love without Hope* Robert Graves
G: *'Me up at does'* e e cummings
H: *Heaven-Haven* Gerard Manley Hopkins
I: *Mother of the Groom* Seamus Heaney
J: *Mind* Richard Wilbur
K: *As Bad as a Mile* Philip Larkin
L: *The Eagle* Alfred, Lord Tennyson

Authorized texts

A: Text 2
B: Text 3
C: Text 3
D: Text 2
E: Text 2
F: Text 1
G: Text 1
H: Text 2
I: Text 1
J: Text 2
K: Text 3
L: Text 1

Bibliography

Beaugrande, R. de and **W. Dressler.** 1981. *Introduction to Text Linguistics.* London: Longman.

Birch, D. 1989. *Language, Literature and Critical Practice: Ways of Analysing Text.* London: Routledge and Kegan Paul.

Burton, D. 1980. *Dialogue and Discourse: A Sociolinguistic Approach to Modern Drama Dialogue and Naturally Occurring Conversation.* London: Routledge and Kegan Paul.

Butler, C. 1984. *Interpretation, Deconstruction and Ideology.* Oxford: Clarendon Press.

Butler, C. and **A. Fowler** (eds.). 1971. *Topics in Criticism.* London: Longman.

Carter, R. A. (ed.). 1982. *Language and Literature: An Introductory Reader in Stylistics.* London: Allen and Unwin.

Carter, R. A. and **M. N. Long.** 1987. *The Web of Words: Exploring Literature through Language.* Cambridge: Cambridge University Press.

Carter, R. A. and **P. Simpson** (eds.). 1989. *Language, Discourse and Literature: An Introductory Reader in Discourse Stylistics.* London: Unwin Hyman.

Cluysenaar, A. 1976. *Introduction to Literary Stylistics.* London: Batsford.

Cole P. and **J. L. Morgan** (eds.). 1975. *Syntax and Semantics Vol. 3: Speech Acts.* New York: Academic Press.

Coulthard, R. M. 1985. *An Introduction to Discourse Analysis.* 2nd edn. London: Longman.

Cox, C. B. and **A. E. Dyson.** 1963. *Modern Poetry: Studies in Practical Criticism.* London: Edward Arnold.

Cox, C. B. and **A. E. Dyson.** 1965. *The Practical Criticism of Poetry: A Textbook.* London: Edward Arnold.

Culler, J. 1981. *The Pursuit of Signs: Semiotics, Literature, Deconstruction.* London: Routledge and Kegan Paul.

Culler, J. 1983. *On Deconstruction: Theory and Criticism after Structuralism.* London: Routledge and Kegan Paul.

Derrida, J. 1967. *De la grammatologie.* Paris: Minuit. Translation: *Of Grammatology.* Baltimore: Johns Hopkins University Press.

Downes, W. A. 1988. 'Discourse and drama: King Lear's "question" to his daughters' in van Peer (ed.) 1988.

Duff, A. and A. Maley. 1990. *Literature.* In the series: *Resource Books for Teachers.* Oxford: Oxford University Press.

Eagleton, T. 1983. *Literary Theory: An Introduction.* Oxford: Basil Blackwell.

Easthope, A. 1983. *Poetry as Discourse.* London: Methuen.

Empson, W. 1961. *Seven Types of Ambiguity.* Harmondsworth: Penguin. First published Chatto and Windus 1930.

Fairclough, N. 1989. *Language and Power.* London: Longman.

Fish, S. 1980. *Is There a Text in This Class? The Authority of Interpretive Communities.* Cambridge, Mass.: Harvard University Press.

Fowler, R. 1981. *Literature as Social Discourse: The Practice of Linguistic Criticism.* London: Batsford.

Fowler, R. 1986. *Linguistic Criticism.* Oxford: Oxford University Press.

Freund, E. 1987. *The Return of the Reader: Reader–Response Criticism.* London: Methuen.

Goffman, E. 1981. *Forms of Talk.* Oxford: Basil Blackwell.

Grice, H. P. 1975. 'Logic and conversation' in Cole and Morgan (eds.) 1975.

Heaney, S. 1990. *The Redress of Poetry.* Oxford: The Clarendon Press.

Jakobson, R. and L. Jones. 1970. *Shakespeare's Verbal Art in 'Th'Expense of Spirit'.* The Hague: Mouton.

Jakobson, R. and C. Levi-Strauss. 1962. ' "Les Chats" de Charles Baudelaire' in *L'Homme 2.* Translation in Lane (ed.) 1970.

Kramsch, C. (forthcoming). *Context and Culture in Language Teaching.* Oxford: Oxford University Press.

Lane, M. (ed.). 1970. *Structuralism: A Reader.* London: Jonathan Cape.

Levinson, S. 1983. *Pragmatics.* Cambridge: Cambridge University Press.

Litz, A. W. and C. MacGowan (eds.). 1991. *William Carlos Williams: Collected Poems Volume I 1909–1939.* London: Paladin/Collins.

Lott, B. M. 1988. 'Language and Literature' (state of the art survey). *Language Teaching* 21/1.

Maley, A. and A. Duff. 1989. *The Inward Ear: Poetry in the Language Classroom.* Cambridge: Cambridge University Press.

McRae, J. 1991. *Literature with a small 'l'.* London: Macmillan.

McRae, J. and L. Pantaleoni. 1986. *Words on the Page.* Oxford: Oxford University Press.

McRae, J. and L. Pantaleoni. 1990. *Chapter & Verse: An Interactive Approach to Literature.* Oxford: Oxford University Press.

Norris, C. 1982. *Deconstruction, Theory and Practice.* London: Methuen.

Quirk, R., S. Greenbaum, G. Leech, and J. Svartvik. 1985. *A Comprehensive Grammar of the English Language.* London: Longman.

Richards, I. A. 1929. *Practical Criticism.* New York: Harcourt Brace and Co.

Scholes, R. 1985. *Textual Power: Literary Theory and the Teaching of English.* New Haven: Yale University Press.

Short, M. H. 1989a. 'Discourse Analysis and the Analysis of Drama' in Carter and Simpson (eds.) 1989.

Short, M. H. (ed.). 1989b. *Reading, Analysing and Teaching Literature.* London: Longman.

Short, M. H. 1990. 'Discourse Analysis in Stylistics and Literature Instruction.' *Annual Review of Applied Linguistics Vol. 11.* Cambridge: Cambridge University Press.

Short, M. H. and W. van Peer. 1989. 'Accident! Stylisticians evaluate: aims and methods of stylistic analysis' in Short (ed.) 1989b.

Sola Pinto, V. de and A. E. Rodway (eds.). 1965. *The Common Muse.* Harmondsworth: Penguin Books.

Sperber, D. and D. Wilson. 1986. *Relevance: Communication and Cognition.* Oxford: Basil Blackwell.

van Peer, W. (ed.). 1988. *The Taming of the Text: Explorations in*

Language, Literature and Culture. London: Routledge.

Whorf, B. L. 1956. *Language, Thought and Reality.* Cambridge Mass.: MIT Press.

Widdowson, H. G. 1975. *Stylistics and the Teaching of Literature.* London: Longman.

Widdowson, H. G. 1984. *Explorations in Applied Linguistics 2.* Oxford: Oxford University Press.

Wimsatt, W. K. 1970. *The Verbal Icon: Studies in the Meaning of Poetry.* London: Methuen. First published by the University of Kentucky Press 1954.

Index

Index of poets

Titles and first lines are given in italics.